THE

GIFT

OF

THE

OUTSIDER

THE

GIFT

OF

THE

OUTSIDER

ALICIA J. AKINS

HARVEST HOUSE PUBLISHERS
EUGENE, OREGON

Cover design by Faceout Studio

Cover image © Yevgen Romanenko / Getty Images

Interior design by Angie Renich, Wildwood Digital Publishing

For bulk, special sales, or ministry purchases, please call 1-800-547-8979. Email: Customerservice@hhpbooks.com

This logo is a federally registered trademark of the Hawkins Children's LLC. Harvest House Publishers, Inc., is the exclusive licensee of this trademark.

The Gift of the Outsider

Copyright © 2023 by Alicia J. Akins
Published by Harvest House Publishers
Eugene, Oregon 97408

www.harvesthousepublishers.com

ISBN 978-0-7369-8423-2 (pbk.)
ISBN 978-0-7369-8424-9 (eBook)

Printed in the United States of America

23 24 25 26 27 28 29 30 31 / BP / 10 9 8 7 6 5 4 3 2 1

To the outsiders who showed me
dimensions of life and faithfulness
only discoverable from the margins.

CONTENTS

FOREWORD

Jen Oshman

I remember the first day I walked my firstborn into her Japanese preschool classroom. She wore the same navy-blue uniform, hat, and indoor shoes as every other child, but she did not wear the same skin, eyes, hair, language, or culture. None of the teachers nor students spoke English, and we did not speak Japanese. My husband and I hugged her, reassured her that everything would be okay, and promised to return several hours later. When I picked her up later that day, I got an earful from her about the many ways Japanese teachers and kids are different from the Americans my daughter was accustomed to. Her first day was foreign in every way.

Our American family lived overseas for years. Our kids attended school in Japan, the Czech Republic, and Germany before we made our way back to the United States, which, according to their passports (but not their hearts), is their home country. They grew up on the outside. We parented from the margins of our communities. Our family had little in common with our neighbors. And now that we're "home" in the US, our outsider status remains because our family forged an identity on different shores.

But I would do it all again. If we were given the opportunity to raise our kids on the outside again, we would jump at the chance. Because although it was always awkward at best, and tearful on the harder days, growing up on the margins was a gift that will never stop producing fruit in my children's lives. They have a global perspective. A big worldview. An awareness of others. Empathy. Eyes to see. These good gifts are harder to find when you're on the inside.

The cultural West, and especially the United States, feels more polarized than ever. And while we do indeed have unique pressures in our age (such as social media and curated news feeds) that invariably push us into corners and silos, humans seeking the company of those who are like themselves—those who agree with them, confirm their views for them, require little from them—is nothing new. Our flesh has always craved stasis and not change, confirmation and not questioning. But is life on the inside what God has for you and me?

In the pages ahead, Alicia Akins encourages and even graciously provokes us who easily get cozy on the inside—the inside circles of our churches, workplaces, cultures, or wherever God has us. She reminds us the poor in the spirit, the meek, those who hunger, and those who are persecuted are the blessed ones. "Blessed are you," Jesus says, "when others revile you and persecute you and utter all kinds of evil against you falsely on my account. Rejoice and be glad, for your reward is great in heaven" (Matthew 5:11-12).

Counter to our culture, flesh, and intuition, the blessings for those who live on the outside are great. And the blessings for those who listen and learn from them promise to be great as well. Outsiders can see what insiders so often miss. They provide us sight where we are blind. They shine light where we may otherwise be in the dark.

I've been back in the American suburbs for seven years now. Most of my community is white, affluent, and politically conservative. And while I still feel a bit off, I am assimilating more every day. I need the views from those on the outside now more than ever. I need my friends of color to help me interpret headlines and how they hit their families differently than they do mine. I need them to talk to me about justice and reform, and I need to see up close what it's like to live in their skin. I need my friends who are immigrants and refugees to show me what it's like to start over—to flee one's government, education, status, loved ones, and comfort and to start anew. I need my friends who are divorced, single, or members of large families to show me how they cling to Christ and his people and depend on us like we are family—because we are. I need my friends who are daily—hourly—walking away from addiction, one step at a time. I need their witness that Christ is enough, no matter what.

My friends on the margins preach a whole sermon with their lives. And I need to hear it. Church, what if we willingly put ourselves on the outside? What if we placed ourselves on the margin? Or, what if we welcomed those on the outside in? What if we trusted Jesus when he says his grace is sufficient for you and me? What if we pursued weakness so that he might be proven strong?

As you turn these pages, turn to the Lord your God. May he use Alicia's wisdom, experience, and words to reveal his heart for the outsider to you. Jesus himself lived on the margins—rejected and slain because he was the Son of God. May he conform you and me more and more into his own image. May he help you and me pursue life and friendships on the outside.

Jen Oshman
Author and speaker

The eye cannot say to the hand, "I have no need of you," nor again the head to the feet, "I have no need of you." On the contrary, the parts of the body that seem to be weaker are indispensable, and on those parts of the body that we think less honorable we bestow the greater honor, and our unpresentable parts are treated with greater modesty, which our more presentable parts do not require. But God has so composed the body, giving greater honor to the part that lacked it, that there may be no division in the body, but that the members may have the same care for one another. If one member suffers, all suffer together; if one member is honored, all rejoice together.

1 Corinthians 12:21-26

INTRODUCTION

Some look to mountains or seas, yet others to the expanse of the sky, but I have always looked to human diversity as the pinnacle of God's creative splendor. The more of its beauty I've understood, the more I've understood how many fail to see its full beauty. My curiosity around difference has grown with each difference encountered.

There are so many ways to be human.

It is not just the world at large that stages God's workmanship. The church—in her unique call to embody the excellencies of Christ, to evidence the power of God, and to unite in mutual submission under one head—also bears the marks of his hands. Yet since time immemorial, insularity, arrogance, comfort, power, and greed have launched sustained attacks against the church in attempts to render her embodiment of Christ's excellencies corrupt, to weaken the influence of God's power, and to foment division.

This book has emerged from a patchwork of joy and sorrow sewn together over the years as I have processed what it means to be different. I share something in common with both those on the margins to whom this book is dedicated and the insiders I seek to convince of the profound beauty of the paradoxes of God's kingdom. With the outsider, I share knowledge of what it's like to navigate systems that, by design, do not work optimally for those in the margins. With the insider, I share knowledge of what it's like to benefit from systems that do. I am both insider and outsider, and I suspect this is true to some degree for most. I also share with each a commitment to glorifying God and enjoying him forever as my chief end,[1] knowing that both those endeavors are enhanced by living faithfully within a united yet diverse community.

We'll begin our journey by coming to an understanding of what I mean when I say "outsider." Then I'll examine four categories of gifts: sight, dependence, freedom, and suffering. Some categories, like sight, are broad enough to encompass a variety of outsider experiences. The others were written with specific outsider groups in mind: those who have disabilities, are chronically ill, or are economically depressed, unmarried, persecuted, or grieving. I'll conclude by illustrating implications of valuing these gifts and those outsiders who steward them well for the church. Each chapter contains reflection questions at the end, some for those who see themselves more as the insider, and some for those who consider themselves more as the outsider.

This book lends its voice to a larger, ongoing discussion about how we—intricately varied as we are—ought to live together in light of the glorious kingdom to which we belong. We've been gifted a messy yet marvelous mission that—when embarked upon faithfully—is sure to stretch us, but more importantly, to result in praise, glory, and honor when Jesus Christ is revealed. Christ alone can claim the credit for fashioning a community where all are recognized as essential and truly treated as such.

When I first sat down to write this book, I feared I would be labeled divisive for raising the issues I wanted to raise. But I cannot be persuaded that the church is not better when we honor *all* its members, when we acknowledge everyone has something to contribute, and when our values are rightly ordered. I have found myself always richer to participate in groups of mixed makeup, regardless of what those lines of difference might be. My prayer is that you would walk away from this book a little more persuaded too.

WHO IS AN OUTSIDER?

God chose what is foolish in the world to shame the wise;
God chose what is weak in the world to shame the strong;
God chose what is low and despised in the world, even
things that are not, to bring to nothing things that are, so
that no human being might boast in the presence of God.

1 Corinthians 1:27-29

Nick speaks with a stutter. Angela uses a wheelchair. Steven was homeschooled as a child but now, as an adult, lives in a big city. Marlene is in her forties and has never married. Bouangern is a new international student in the US. Dan has recently gotten swept up in replacement theory. Alex is an undocumented immigrant. Jasmine, a Black woman, attends a predominantly white church. Mariella is a first-generation college student. John is a recovering addict. Wayne is the only man who works in his department. The Moores struggle with infertility. Sarah Kate is politically conservative but moved to Seattle for work. Terry has lived for 30 years in his quickly gentrifying neighborhood, where nearly all his neighbors are recent transplants.

Liz and Michael are the only white people on their block in an "up-and-coming" neighborhood. Stephanie suffers from chronic illness. Maxwell is neurodivergent.

What do these people have in common?

The Terrors of the Outside

At one time or another, and to varying degrees, the people just described have all felt like outsiders or feared becoming one. For some, trying to recall a time when they *didn't* feel like an outsider proves more difficult than pinpointing a specific situation in which they did. Whether what sets them apart from the majority is visible or something derived from personal choice or background, their experience of being different is likely similar: feelings of discomfort, isolation, or anxiety, or the sense of being unseen. Perhaps they want nothing more than to minimize the felt difference between themselves and others as they attempt to acclimate to a new culture (even if that culture is just a new church). Maybe they carry a sense of loss, having once been on the inside. If they're at all like me, they've struggled with how their difference might limit them and frustrate their ambitions. Maybe they walk on eggshells, unable to fully be themselves for fear of offending the dominant group or exposing themselves as outsiders and facing marginalization. However else they may differ from each other, in these ways, they can relate.

An outsider is a person or group of people who differ from those around them in one or more ways that are meaningful either to them or to the prevailing immediate culture. Their difference may be based on life stage, socioeconomic status, education, circumstances, culture (ethnic, regional, national), ability, interests, or identity. Their experience of being on the outside may be episodic or permanent.

If mapped as concentric rings, insiders—those sharing the most meaningful traits with each other—would make up the innermost ring. Outsiders would fall at various distances from the center based on a variety of quantitative and qualitative factors. In how many ways does the individual differ? How visible is their difference? To what extent does their difference prevent them from full participation in the wider group? How much weight does the group or individual put on sameness in general or on that specific difference? What legal protections or lack thereof accompany that category of difference? To what extent are freedoms, power, and influence limited or is dignity denied as a result of the difference?

In C.S. Lewis's essay "The Inner Ring," he writes, "I believe that in all men's lives at certain periods, and in many men's lives at all periods between infancy and extreme old age, one of the most dominant elements is the desire to be inside the local Ring and the terror of being left outside." *Terror* may seem like a strong word, but some go to quite drastic lengths to maintain or gain privileged positions. Most people vie for the inside. When being on the inside means being known, seen, and accommodated, who wouldn't want that? If we had our way, we'd avoid the outside at all costs.

My Outsider Story

It seems everywhere you turn, diversity is discussed. The discussions I hear most often revolve around racial diversity—which I, too, am a huge proponent of—but diversity is, well, more diverse than that. I am not limiting this exploration to racial differences, nor to only those differences I've experienced. I'm casting a wider net than most in how I think about outsiders because the experience is more widespread than we tend to think.

I was born in Kansas to Air Force parents, and soon thereafter we relocated to Japan for a couple of years before spending five glorious, harsh winters in Michigan. My family was one of a handful of Black families in each of these locations. I hadn't thought much of being different until, after sharing with my older sister that I had a crush on a white neighbor, she told me white boys didn't like Black girls.

In fourth grade, I found myself in Virginia, where I finally got to interact with more Black kids. It was not a positive experience for me. My Black peers regularly gave me the cold shoulder or accused me of "acting white" when I was just being me. One Black classmate "befriended" me just to give me "Black lessons" during lunch. Apparently, my other—white—friends were all wrong and I spoke "too proper." I wondered why I needed to change for my own people to accept me. At least openly, white people didn't point out my differences, and as far as I knew, they didn't seem to punish me for them either.

Neither I nor my interests were particularly popular. I was that kid in school who would pre-emptively ask the teacher if I could work alone on group projects—not because I was an introvert, but because I was scarred from not being chosen so often. Music was my passion, and my favorite genres were alternative, classical, and Latin—choices the rest of my family couldn't have been less excited about. On Sunday afternoons, a local radio station would play Latin music. I would book it from the church sanctuary to the car after Sunday services so I could catch some of it before my sisters caught up and asked me to turn it off.

In high school, I went on scholarship to summer arts camps where most campers came from affluent backgrounds. Before then, I'd mostly mixed and mingled with those from the same socioeconomic status as my family. I still remember sitting in a Northwestern University dorm listening to other campers talk about places in Europe they'd visited on vacation as casually as if they were destinations right down the street. At a different camp, I'd lie in bed listening to the others talk about their favorite artisanal breads and cheeses when I only knew white, wheat, and cheddar. That summer, I was grateful for our camp uniforms— corduroy knickers, knee socks, and polos—because they made it less obvious who was well-off. I felt no love for overt signals of social status.

After high school, I said goodbye to the suburbs of southeastern Virginia to study music education at Rutgers—a state school in New Jersey—where many students either knew each other or at least shared a Jersey identity. The rest of my family had or would attend historically Black colleges. I had a Black roommate briefly at the beginning of my freshman year. We'd talked over the phone once during the summer, but when she met me in person, she said, "I thought you'd be Blacker." Perhaps I should have warned her. I played two less popular instruments, viola and tuba, and was one of two Black string players in the orchestra and the only woman tuba player in the marching band.

As a departure from my traditional Black church roots, I joined a predominantly white campus ministry. Even though I was well liked, I sometimes felt culturally and politically like an outsider. Once a group of us went to a state fair, and I grabbed a button from a Democratic politician's booth and pinned it to my shirt. One friend glared at me nearly the whole car ride home before he could no longer contain himself, exclaiming, "I don't see how you can be a Democrat and call yourself a Christian." But as far as I could otherwise judge from our fruit, political affiliation bore no direct appreciable impact on our spiritual maturity.

Other times, my difference played out in small interactions like retreat games or conversations about childhood memories and "classic" performers and TV shows I'd never heard of. I met my first boyfriend through that ministry—a white guy who at least partially proved my sister wrong. His mother thrust me quickly back to reality; after our first meeting, she described me as "lazy like all Black people" because I'd told her I had a chance to perform at Carnegie Hall but was considering turning it down due to other commitments. I wasn't Black enough by Black standards, but still managed to be too Black by some white ones.

After college, I moved to China, my first stint abroad since I was three, and threw myself into a new language and culture. Although I was even further from belonging to the majority there, I felt a strange sense of relief to not be surrounded by the white majority of whom I'd begun to grow weary. I moved to a new city each of the three years I lived there. In the smallest of those cities, I was one of two Black residents out of a population of a million. I'd chosen that location because of a university there specifically for Chinese ethnic minorities.

The experience of minorities in other countries intrigued me. In the mornings on my way to class, I had to bike past a field where soldiers trained. Every day a different one would point at me and yell in Chinese, "Look! It's an African!" Their shocked expressions after I yelled back in Chinese, "I'm not African, I'm American!" are forever etched in my memory.

I stuck out more in China than anywhere else I'd lived, but I approached Chinese people's curiosity about my difference as an opportunity to be an ambassador for Black people. I knew that apart from Obama, Oprah, and Kobe Bryant, Chinese exposure to Black people was limited to either news headlines about our criminality or movies depicting us as underachieving students or athletes in need of white saviors. It became my mission to ensure my every interaction with them would send them home with a radically different picture of what it meant to be Black.

My experience in China unlocked within me an unapologetic embrace of being different. After repatriating to the States, I joined an Asian American church in Boston that significantly expanded my understanding of the Bible's stance on justice—a topic largely unbroached in my previous church experiences. I was a long way from my college church, where they taught that a missions trip wasn't a missions trip if you only met material needs. This church held it wasn't a true missions trip if you neglected those physical needs. The discomfort of that tension kept me there. I considered it good to be a little uncomfortable at church. I busied myself with Japanese classes since I wanted to keep in touch with my non-English-speaking Japanese friend. She and I moved away from China at the same time and I worried one or both of us would forget Chinese and have no way to communicate. I also joined the bhangra dance club. My house of four women was multicultural: one white Christian, one Jewish, one Indian, and me.

Two years later, I was accepted into graduate school and moved to Seattle to study China and museums. Having once been completely ignorant about the beauty, depth, and diversity of the region myself,

I wanted to teach people about that part of the world. Outside of my years in China, Seattle was the first time I really felt like a religious minority. I was the only Christian in either of my programs and frequently watched classmates demonstrating open antagonism toward Christianity. I attended a Korean American church, where I was adopted by the most amazing family who let me spend school breaks and holidays like Thanksgiving with them. One year, after finishing the Thanksgiving meal with *haraboji, halmoni,* and a collection of aunts, uncles, and cousins, a group of us were watching TV in the living room. A crime show came on, featuring police arresting Black people doing their best to resist. I immediately felt embarrassed.

After finishing graduate school, despite hating hot weather and bugs and adoring big cities, a dream work opportunity took me—with no connections—to Laos, a tiny landlocked country in Southeast Asia often eclipsed by its neighbors Thailand and Vietnam. Drawn once more by my interest in what it was like to be a minority somewhere else, I worked at a museum highlighting the different ethnic groups in Laos, mostly alongside local men with just a high school education. I was the only Black person living in my town. Because staff meetings were mostly conducted in Lao, I added another language to my growing collection. My second year, I began studying Thai. That year, I also lived with my closest friend, a Vietnamese woman from Hanoi, as well as a Canadian woman. I called myself "the poor expat"; compared to my Lao peers, I earned a lot, but compared with other foreigners, I made very, very little.

When my contract ended, Washington, DC, became home, and I first worked for two years at an Asian art museum where I was the only person of color on my team. This time, I joined a majority white church with more politically conservative members than in my previous churches and got to explore more dimensions of difference. After my first small group—folks I felt a strong affinity with because of shared experiences living or studying abroad—disbanded three years in, I intentionally joined the least diverse—and most unlike me—small group I could find. I thought it would be good for me to have my own assumptions challenged and to find common ground with people with whom I thought I had little but Jesus in common. I also thought it would be good for them. "Everyone benefits from difference" had become my mindset.

Four years ago, I embarked on a master's program at a theologically conservative seminary where, as a Black, politically liberal woman, I stand out from most of my classmates. I'm toward the lower end of the income scale compared to most of my peers. I'm also in my late thirties and happily unmarried, while my friends have nearly all coupled off and begun their own families. As a result, friendships dynamics have begun to shift. Three years ago, I began to suffer from as-yet undiagnosed health problems. To top it all off, I run in nerd circles but have never seen any *Star Wars*, *Star Trek*, or *Harry Potter* movies, nor have I heard the soundtrack to *Hamilton*.

In terms of race, socioeconomic and marital status, nationality, religion, interests, politics, gender, and life experience, I'm often on the outside. Sometimes being an outsider has been beyond my control; I had no say in my race or gender, and no control over my childhood experience moving around. Sometimes it was a consequence of my choice to pursue certain interests or communities. Other times I sought it out, as with my choices of universities, churches, and living abroad.

No matter how being an outsider has come about for me, I've always learned from it. Over time, I moved from insecurity about my difference to neutrality to recognizing the value in it and letting it better me. It has taught me about the bigness of God, the closeness of God, the power of God, and the person- and circumstance-specific care of God. I have grown in how I view myself, where my value does and doesn't come from, what I was made for, and how to reconsider the sand under my house I'd mistaken for rocks.

During a particularly trying season of life, I wrote to a friend, "Are all stations and circumstances that illuminate the true nature of grace a gift? Since Paul boasts in his weaknesses and hardships because they facilitate his most powerful encounters with grace (2 Corinthians 12:8-10), then are all things gifts that bring to rest on us Christ's power?"

It was my very differences that convinced me of God's sovereignty over things like the time and place in which I lived and the family into which I was born. The realization that God wasn't just able to work for my good *despite* my race, but *because* of it, deepened my faith. And with every new dimension of difference granted to me and that I've observed in others, my understanding of God's grace and the staggering beauty of his kingdom deepens.

In *The Outside Edge*, Robert Kelsey claims that being a true outsider is exclusively negative: "There's nothing inherently enabling about this situation, no matter what the view of fashionable commentators. There are no advantages. There's no *edge* to being on the edge."[1] A bleak outlook indeed.

But if I could go back and reverse any of my outsider experiences for the inside, I wouldn't. All the privileges and benefits of the inside could not tempt me to part with all I've gained from being on the outside. I would not trade discomfort for comfort, difference for sameness. A world where I don't see what I now see, feel what I now feel, or know what I now know is unimaginable. I am fully convinced the world and church need certain things for their flourishing that sprout only from seeds of difference.

Even with all its seeming disadvantages, being an outsider comes with benefits—as overlooked and underappreciated as they may be. Though my experiences have been wide-ranging, I know enough to understand they don't encompass the full scope of the outsider experience.

A Better Endgame

We love rooting for underdogs, whether in sports or business. Rags-to-riches stories also have wide appeal. We make heroes of those who rise above humble beginnings to "make something" of themselves.

But here's where Christians diverge from this way of thinking. Certainly, the story of the Bible is one of nothings—the least of all nations—finding themselves undeservedly at the center of God's favor. Throughout Scripture, being outnumbered was a source of anxiety for Israel. Every time they faced an enemy, they cowered because of their size (Numbers 13:25-33; Deuteronomy 2:10; Deuteronomy 7:1; Judges 7; 2 Kings 6:15-17). Being small both in number and size meant they were especially vulnerable to enemies. They were ripe for defeat—yet still chosen by the Most High.

God's people are not those who live to "make something" of themselves. Rather, we live to be made—through the immeasurable greatness of resurrection power—like the very best of somethings: Christ. Self-mortifying, neighbor-edifying, right-forfeiting, enemy-blessing heirs of grace.

So, if growing in Christlikeness, being carriers of his scent throughout a decaying world, and striving to make the realities of his kingdom visible in your living and loving are not your goals for these few precious days you've been given, you may struggle to appreciate what follows in the pages ahead. You will find no secrets about how to crush it at work or win friends or gain access to the inside. This is not that sort of book.

Reaching the inside—that coveted inner ring—is not my endgame; it wasn't Christ's. What you will find instead is a way of thinking about the cards we've been dealt and the experiences we've had as raw materials God can use to exhibit his all-surpassing power. What most benefits us, individually and as the church, is what moves us closer to our goal of becoming worshipers with a singular boast who make nothing of ourselves and everything of God—becoming faithful disciples and proof of his power.

Prosperity's Unread Warning Label

As we pine after the inside, we assume that smoother and easier always means better. This is not the case. Far too often, the dangers and temptations of the inside are glossed over to our detriment. Insiders may unknowingly inflict harm on others and continue in unchallenged sin, harming themselves and missing out on the grace flowering in dark corners of their hearts. Smooth and easy come with their own risks.

Not every outsider will necessarily possess every gift we will examine. Rather, you can think of it as ease of acquisition, like learning a language by immersion rather than in a distant classroom setting. Certain circumstances lend themselves more naturally to certain ends. For example, when Jesus speaks of the rich young ruler (Matthew 19:23-24), he doesn't say it is impossible for the rich to enter his kingdom, just that it is more difficult for them than it is for a camel to pass through the eye of a needle. Some rich will be in heaven, but they will have overcome the worldward gravitational pull of their wealth. While viewed from the world's perspective, their wealth is an asset; from a heavenly perspective, it is a liability—one that those of lesser means do not have or have in lesser degrees. Power, influence, and privilege (in all its forms) may also be liabilities.

Sure, some people without power, influence, and privilege still orient their lives around the attainment and worship of these things. But the challenges for those who already possess them are real. The closer we get to being able to explain away the good things in our lives through our own sense of self-sufficiency, the greater the temptation to worship ourselves rather than God. When Israel finally entered the Promised Land after wandering in the desert for 40 years, they switched from being fed by God directly through manna that miraculously appeared to cultivating and harvesting the land for food (Joshua 5:12). During that transition, God instituted a festival. Its purpose was to ensure they remembered he was the God who continued to feed them even as they worked the ground—*not* a God who fed them and then left them to feed themselves in Canaan. Once our hands hit the ground, God must contend with our own sense of resourcefulness for credit.

In Ezekiel's allegory of the unfaithful wife (Ezekiel 16:1-58), God describes Israel as a woman he discovered bloody on the street after her birth, a woman whom he cleaned, clothed, and adorned with jewels. Later, that woman came to trust in her own beauty. God said,

> And I put a ring on your nose and earrings in your ears and a beautiful crown on your head. Thus you were adorned with gold and silver, and your clothing was of fine linen and silk and embroidered cloth. You ate fine flour and honey and oil. You grew exceedingly beautiful and advanced to royalty. And your renown went forth among the nations because of your beauty, for it was perfect through the splendor that I had bestowed on you, declares the Lord GOD. But you trusted in your beauty and played the whore (verses 12-15).

This is often us, trusting in gifts bestowed. The temptation for those of us who came to know Christ as kids is to sanitize our conversion story. In our memories, there was no time when we were abhorred and wallowing in our own blood (Ezekiel 16:5-6). As far back as we can remember, we have been adorned—but in reality, we are still being cleaned and clothed.

God desired and provided prosperity for his people, but he knew abundance carried the risk of losing the plot, forgetting his hand, and drifting into idolatry of the very goods he'd blessed them with. This holds true for us too. Satan sought to capitalize on the natural tendency of humankind when he sought permission to test Job, saying: "Does Job fear God for no reason? Have you not put a hedge around him and his house and all that he has, on every side? You have blessed the work of his hands, and his possessions have increased in the land. But stretch out your hand and touch all that he has, and he will curse you to your face" (Job 1:9-11).

Was Job in it for God? Or the well-hedged, enviable life he lived?

When we are comfortable, provided for, healthy, approved by our peers, enjoying systems that work in our favor, or in possession of what we most desire, it is hardest to discern the truth of our love for and commitment to God. Often, as goes the ease goes our love. When life goes sideways or we face opposition, out comes doubt. *Is God good? Can he be trusted? Is he still the good, good father I sang about last week?*

We think too little of the dangers—often stealth—of easy and comfortable Christian lives. In some ways, we may be hampered by privilege and prosperity. The very things we think help us advance may actually hold us back. Theologian Charles Hodge writes in his commentary on 1 Corinthians, "The things which elevate man in the world, knowledge, influence, rank, are not the things which lead to God and salvation."[2] We fail to value plotlines for our lives that put our beliefs to the test—plotlines that take us, like Job, from hearing of God by the hearing of the ear to seeing him with our eyes (Job 42:5). That force our genuine convictions into the open. Steadfastness, while admirable in others, pales in comparison to prosperity when it comes to what we desire for ourselves, even though steadfastness is the goal of our faith (James 1:3-4).

Yet prosperity is not always the marker of health we think it is. Time and again, people in the Bible confessed they envied or almost envied the at ease and prosperous (Job 21:7-34; Psalm 73:3-16; Jeremiah 12:1-2). Time and again, God assured them no correlation existed between what they had and his pleasure with them. It is not that God does not want us to prosper, but rather that prosperity comes with a warning label we rarely read.

I won't demonize the young, the wealthy, the powerful, etc.—God has great plans for them too. In and of themselves, youth, wealth, and power are not evil, but they do come with powerful temptations that age, poverty, and vulnerability might not. Let us exercise our holy imaginations and reconsider the dignity and strengths of outsiders.

Part of the gift of being an outsider is being able to live unencumbered (or at least, less encumbered) by the distortions and self-deceptions that come from whatever form of wealth—financial, relational, reputational—we are prone to define ourselves by. The insider is at higher risk of unwittingly making their possessions—both material and immaterial—their masters. And, as Matthew 6:24 says, "No one can serve two masters."

The Value of Difference

A value of difference unique to the church is that it presents a canvas upon which God can paint one of its most distinctive features: unity. There is power in finding unity where we least expect it. As differences increase, we expect the opportunities for division to increase as well. But God makes the startling possible: We can discover unity in diversity—even where histories of mistreatment and mistrust run deep and the potential for marginalization and neglect run high.

One summer as a VBS volunteer, we played a game where we split into groups. Some members were assigned roles such as being a baby or a sick or elderly person requiring extra help. Then we were told to complete an obstacle course and finish together. The spectacle of total depravity that followed was sad yet unsurprising. Those without special roles rushed ahead, concerned only with their race and their finish time—even if it meant their team ultimately lost. Few wanted to be weighed down by those who might cost them their individual lead. Players demonstrated little interest in unity because it moved them down the leaderboard.

Had there been no special roles or had the object of the game been different, an every-man-for-himself, survival-of-the fittest mentality would have made sense. But that game would be completely divorced from the character and aims of God's kingdom and its witness in the world. In our call to Christ, we are called to each other. In *Life Together*, Dietrich Bonhoeffer writes,

> Without Christ we also would not know our brother, nor could we come to him. The way is blocked by our own ego. Christ opened up the way to God and to our brother. Now Christians can live with one another in peace; they can love and serve one another; they can become one. But they can continue to do so only by way of Jesus Christ.[3]

Difference also expresses the vastness of God's beauty and wisdom. We are prone to looking at the surface of things, to judging people by their utility, to settling into rigid ways of thinking, to valuing the inconsequential, and to dismissing the invaluable. But the innumerable ways of being and speaking and thinking that exist serve as a witness to the unfathomable imagination of our Creator. Would a bald mountain range dare say to one covered in trees, "Because you are covered in trees, you are less majestic," or a bird-of-paradise blossom say to a magnolia, "Because your colors are not as vibrant as mine, you are not beautiful"? Not at all! And we are just as much the proclamations of his handiwork as the skies, fields, and seas.

Our difference is also sometimes the very thing God intends to use to mold us into his image. It may not be our preferred method of learning, but difference provides us with natural opportunities to see God's hand—and to see others—in ways we otherwise could not. Status quo and sameness cannot fully teach us about his depths. We are valuable apart from what we do, who sees and desires us, where our limits fall, and where we rank in this world of distorted weights and measures.

Outsiders in the Body of Christ

The body politic metaphor Paul employs throughout his letters has long served to illustrate diverse members of a political or social community working together toward shared goals. When Paul speaks of the body of Christ, he invokes and inverts that image. Whereas in its most common usage, the members lower on the social hierarchy are rallied to work toward the interests of those higher on the hierarchy, Paul is arguing for deference to those of lower position. Anglican theologian Anthony C. Thiselton writes,

> It is an affront to Christ if a self-effacing or vulnerable Christian is made to feel second class or alienated, perhaps because he or she does not have what others see as the "right" gifts. It is a betrayal if such a person reaches the point of saying, "I do not *belong* to the body" (1 Corinthians 12:15).

To drive home this principle Paul borrows, *but also then reverses*, an application of the imagery of the body long known and used in Greco-Roman politics and rhetoric. From the fourth and fifth centuries B.C. through the first century up to the second, Plato, Plutarch, and Epictetus (contemporary with Paul) used the image of the body to promote the need for harmony where there was diversity of status. The Roman historian Livy narrates an appeal by the senator Menenius Agrippa to rebel workers on strike to resume work (*Ab Urbe Conditu 2.32*). He appeals to the interdependence of the "body" of the city to urge that the workers or slaves must provide food for the governing classes. Paul reverses the thrust of this appeal, *transposing it into an appeal to "the strong" to value "the weak" or despised.*[4]

The church, to its glory, is comprised of varied peoples with varied gifts. Yet, whether we'd like to admit it or not, even here we find evidence of the adoption of social distinctions more closely mirroring the culture than God's kingdom. The culture Paul was addressing in Corinth was composed of individuals under the same spell as the larger Greco-Roman culture, which ruthlessly sought status and honor.[5] While we may not admit that love of honor and status is the animating force of our lives, let either be lost and we are overcome with shame.

The gospel holds out the hope of existing within a culture where honor, dignity, and belonging are not a product of pedigree, family of birth, being chosen by others, color of skin, income, ability, or what one can produce. But we do not reflect God or the true culture of his kingdom when people who are visible and dear to him are invisible or inconsequential to us. We fail to comprehend the magnitude of his purposes and grace as well as the utter perfection of his world-frustrating wisdom.

We are presented, as members of a diverse church, with opportunities to affirm the dignity, beauty, and value of its every member. We are challenged to rethink our boast as God pursues, chooses, and lavishes his grace upon those whose only boast is him. And we each must face these uncomfortable truths: As far as God's kingdom is concerned, we were chosen despite ourselves. No one will inherit the kingdom who believes they are entitled to it. Our weakness carries more cachet with God than our strength.

A New Kind of Opting Outside

The impulse to be on the inside isn't always wrong. In my two stints living in Asia as an adult, I dove headfirst into two cultures that couldn't be further from my own and did my best to acclimate. This meant more than learning the language. I tried making Paul's aim to become all things to all people my own:

> For though I am free from all, I have made myself a servant to all, that I might win more of them. To the Jews I became as a Jew, in order to win Jews. To those under the law I became as one under the law (though not being myself under the law) that I might win those under the law. To those outside the law I became as one outside the law (not being outside the law of God but under the law of Christ) that I might win those outside the law. To the weak I became weak, that I might win the weak. I have become all things to all people, that by all means I might save some. I do it all for the sake of the gospel, that I may share with them in its blessings (1 Corinthians 9:19-23).

Meeting people where they are for the sake of the gospel is commendable. Of course, I inevitably stuck out as a Black woman. No matter how proficient I became in the languages or how well I adapted to doing as the locals did, my outsider status remained painted on my skin.

Loved Deep and Wide

The identity of outsiders is not foremost as victims but as recipients of special grace. This puts us in league not necessarily with those whose lives overflow with material blessings, but with Paul: "afflicted in every way, but not crushed; perplexed, but not driven to despair" (2 Corinthians 4:8). We are witnesses of and to the surpassing power of God, a greater badge of honor than summer homes, loving spouses, healthy bodies, and lives of utmost comfort.

Paul's prayer for the Christians in Ephesus to have the strength to comprehend the breadth and length and height and depth of the love of Christ (Ephesians 3:14-21) is also my prayer for you. That, for the outsider, as you let the truths of God's heart for you seep into the deepest and hardest-to-reach corners of your identity, you would ascertain new levels of its depths. For the insider, that as you watch the same love God has for you extend across the widest of margins, you would better comprehend its breadth. And that we together would marvel at God's expectation-shattering love.

Our Journey Together

Some may accuse me of having an overly rosy picture of life on the outside. Or of glorifying something that, in some cases, might better be grieved. It's true; sometimes the mere existence of an outside bears bitter witness to a broken world. I know well that it comes with its share of challenges—real, big, heartbreaking, and in some cases, life-threatening. But it holds as much potential for growth and self-discovery as for pain.

Part of my aim in writing this book is to stimulate self-reflection. The reflection questions at the end of each chapter present a chance to step back from being defensive or reactionary and think soberly about ourselves. Another goal is to share some of my journey from viewing differences as burdens to recognizing them as gifts as I engaged God through them. I also want to encourage those still burdened by their difference to see how they can be bettered by it. But more than anything, I want us, whether insiders or outsiders, to see Christ more clearly and to delight in the paradoxical vision he has for his body. To see with fresh eyes its goodness and godliness and to seek anew its peace and purity.

Our journey in these pages will take us deeper into the gifts that come with being on the outside. Some of these gifts will be general to all kinds of outsiders, whereas others may be more specific. Outsiderness endows its possessor with a special ability to see what can only be seen from a distance, with a field of vision wide enough to see the margins, with a higher tolerance for discomfort, and with a sensitivity to others' experiences that insiders may lack. The Bible speaks to the unique contributions of outsiders to God's kingdom, to God's special care for outcasts, to the special honor given to parts of the body that lack it, and to the supremacy of faith. The gifts of the outsider require thoughtful embrace both by the outsiders themselves and those predisposed to see the outside position as one of weakness.

When Jesus took on flesh, he embarked on the life of an outsider. Whether we've always been outsiders, are looking to become one, or just want to better love the ones in our midst, he knows our path. Christ gives us courage, conviction, and perspective the world cannot, and we look to his example. Humbled by a sacrifice that undid our alienation, we honor everything his blood bought for us. As people of the cross—being built together with Christ as our cornerstone—division does not become us.

Reflection Questions

1. When you think of an outsider, what comes to mind?

   _____

   _____

   _____

   _____

2. Which, if any, of the individuals at the opening of this chapter can you relate to?

   _____

   _____

   _____

   _____

3. If you consider yourself a seasoned outsider, what has that experience taught you?

   _____

   _____

   _____

   _____

4. If you consider yourself a sporadic outsider, what is your normal reaction or response to situations that draw attention to your outsiderness?

   _____

   _____

   _____

   _____

5. Who are the "outsiders" in your life?

_____

_____

_____

_____

6. Read Colossians 3:11. If Paul were writing to the church today, what divisions do you think he would highlight? If he were writing to your specific church, what might he point out?

_____

_____

_____

_____

7. In your culture, where are the loci of shame and stigma when it comes to difference and division? Where is it okay to be different? When does difference carry shame?

_____

_____

_____

_____

GIFTS OF SIGHT

Outsiders view insiders, other outsiders,
and the world differently. The following
chapters look at these gifts of sight.

2

VISION
Seeing the Inside

The heart is deceitful above all things.

JEREMIAH 17:9

Culture is a bit like Magic Eye pictures. You think you know what you're looking at, but no sooner than you hold that page full of repeated patterns out at a distance does a new image emerge. Depth perception makes a world of difference.

I thought I knew what it was to be an American. Yet it took moving overseas—holding the image out a distance, if you will—for the borders of my Americanness to come into view. Distance often best cures shortsightedness, distorted thinking, or a lack of self-awareness. It wasn't just the distance, though, that affected my thinking. It was also the contrast of seeing myself next to both expats from other countries and locals that refined my understanding of what exactly an American was and what made us distinct. Americanness emerged from the background of once familiar repeated patterns. Turns out, moving to the outside helps one see the inside more clearly.

Privilege took on new dimensions. The concept is so often framed by race or by gender in the US that, as a double minority (Black and female), privilege had felt outside of my experience. Living as an American abroad forced me to see how privilege could be at work undetected by its possessor. Being an English speaker, the strength of the dollar, my access to education and high-quality (albeit expensive) healthcare, and my well-educated parents afforded me a certain amount of privilege, both globally and domestically, I hadn't before considered.

Now that we've closed in on what I mean by *outsider* in the first chapter, the next three chapters look at general gifts outsiders may possess regardless of the kind of outsider experience they've had. Under the umbrella of "sight," these gifts look at insider vision, perspective, and empathy.

You Are the Man

In the infamous David and Bathsheba story, the prophet Nathan visited David after Uriah's death and David's marriage to Bathsheba. He shared with David a story that mirrored what David had done without making the connection explicit.

> There were two men in a certain city, the one rich and the other poor. The rich man had very many flocks and herds, but the poor man had nothing but one little ewe lamb, which he had bought. And he brought it up, and it grew up with him and with his children. It used to eat of his morsel and drink from his cup and lie in his arms, and it was like a daughter to him. Now there came a traveler to the rich man, and he was unwilling to take one of his own flock or herd to prepare for the guest who had come to him, but he took the poor man's lamb and prepared it for the man who had come to him (2 Samuel 12:1-4).

David responded in outrage.

David was able to be convicted and see the error of his ways thanks to the rebuke of a prophet. However, *how* Nathan rebuked David is worth noting. I sometimes wonder how David would have responded had Nathan confronted him head-on. We'll never know. Instead, it was the distance Nathan created that allowed David to see himself and his actions with objective clarity. Distance brought David to his knees. Knowledge of oneself is invaluable. The Bible urges us to think of ourselves "with sober judgment" (Romans 12:3). Meanwhile, our egos and self-deceiving hearts get in the way. Proverbs 26:12 says "there is more hope for a fool" than a man "wise in his own eyes." Proverbs 28:26 says, "Whoever trusts in his own mind is a fool, but he who walks in wisdom will be delivered." According to these verses, the wise are not those who consider themselves so, and the self-assured walk hopelessly in darkness. Outsiders—and a little humility—can help.

We usually look to people close to us to get a read on how we're received and what kind of people we are, but we should also consider the insight we could gain from those who don't know us well. Having people who will see you from a variety of angles in your circle and in your church is helpful. Outsiders help us see the things we're least likely to notice in ourselves and our communities, and they can provide a dispassionate perspective on how we're perceived. Part of the reason that distance helps is because proximity hurts. Proximity can create a barrier to thinking of ourselves objectively. The emotional stakes are higher when you're evaluating or viewing a group to which you belong. But an openness to hearing from outsiders is a sign of humility. Proverbs 15:31-32 says, "The ear that listens to life-giving reproof will dwell among the wise. Whoever ignores instruction despises himself, but he who listens to reproof gains intelligence." Surrounding ourselves with other insiders may limit what we're able to see about ourselves. Some of the most helpful, life-giving reproof may not always come from people like us.

Church of the Insider

In the church of the insider, everyone assumes their concerns are universal, exhaustive, and paramount. Fringe concerns, when they do arise, are not addressed, as they do not have the critical mass worth expending the effort to find a solution. Cultural references are assumed to be meaningful to all. They think the most important questions the Bible answers are the ones they ask. Shared sin patterns become culturally acceptable—so you will not hear sermons on those. The status quo is sacred. Groupthink is worshiped over shalom, and challenges to it are viewed as threats, not opportunities. Strengths abound. Weaknesses are rare and downplayed at every turn. "Overall" matters more than "worst-case" because, the thinking goes, *the impact of worst cases only affects a few.* Unless, that is, the worst case affects an influential insider. Then it becomes paramount.

Sound familiar?

Such a church is plagued by the paradox of people not seeing themselves because they *only* see themselves. This happens not just in racially or culturally homogenous churches. The same holds true for any group of people who share common traits. Even as we, in our modern age, have the widest, most convenient exposure to other cultures and ways of thinking, silos remain ubiquitous. To keep from getting swept up in their dangerous undercurrents, we must remain vigilant. A friend once described insider culture at my church, and when I insisted there was no inner ring, he exclaimed, "That's how you know you're part of it."

Like Fish in Water

As part of a commencement speech, author David Foster Wallace shared a story about fish that don't know they're in water: "There are these two young fish swimming along and they happen to meet an older fish swimming the other way, who nods at them and says 'Morning, boys. How's the water?' And the two young fish swim on for a bit, and then eventually one of them looks over at the other and goes 'What the [heck] is water?'"[1]

We might not see the totality of a culture from outside it, but we can see things others take for granted or don't even realize. Every culture has systems, traditions, or beliefs that are invisible to insiders and immediately obvious to outsiders. When we invite people who aren't like us to speak into our lives, we are living out the belief that the thoughts and opinions of outsiders matter. At the same time, we also do ourselves a favor by welcoming valuable new perspectives.

The very first conversation I had with someone when I moved to China served as a perfect foretaste of the acculturation to come. When she asked me how old I was, I gave my age and she gave hers, leading to the pleasant discovery that we were the same age! In solidarity, I asked her, "You were born in '83, too?" But she hadn't been, nor had she been born in '82 or '84. To my surprise, her birth year was off from mine by two.

"So, aren't you 20, not 21?" I asked. All my life I'd thought there was one way to calculate age, not realizing that I had interpreted a product of my specific culture as a universal norm. I would never have thought to question it, but that day I learned that in China, when discussing age, you're one year old at birth and you give your age based on the age you will turn that year, even if your birthday has not passed. I began throwing myself birthday parties for multiple ages at a time.

The Arm Bends Inward

Many factors contribute to outsiders seeing the inside with special clarity. In addition to distance, partiality also clouds how we view other people, situations, and the world itself.

An old Korean proverb translates literally as "the arm bends inward," meaning that people always favor those closest to them. It is human nature to want to see yourself and the groups to which you belong in the best light. It's perfectly natural for us to be the most emotionally invested in ourselves and the things within our circle of concern. And yet, "perfectly natural" is not always what God asks of us. Deuteronomy 10:12 tells us, "For the LORD your God is God of gods and Lord of lords, the great, the mighty, and the awesome God, who is not partial and takes no bribe." His arm doesn't bend inward like ours. To be like him, we must have our arms fixed.

For this renewal of our perspective to begin, we must first recognize the direction our arms bend and their need to be fixed. This might be an unpopular opinion, but this is also true for outsiders. Even when we are on the outside, our arms bend too. Some may say the assumptions marginalized people make about others are fine—not so. Outsiders are also accountable to God for the content of their hearts. We cannot say it is the doer of wrong only and not the sufferer of it who will be judged, though along different lines. For example, when I was a kid, a common excuse for snapping at a sibling was: "She made me do it!"—but that excuse won't work with God. I wasn't responsible for my sibling's actions, but I was responsible for my response both in deed and in thought. God left us detailed instructions on how to treat those who mistreat and misunderstand us, even setting an example for us. We all must examine our assumptions and confess what we find to God.

A part of the reason I joined that one small group at my church was because I knew I was biased against certain kinds of people who were in that group. My heart needed to change. I thought it would be good for me to worship with them, to dig into Scripture with them, to hear their prayer requests every week, to break bread and celebrate life milestones with them. We need to be careful not to perpetuate the same sins committed against us in our hearts toward others.

Favoritism

Classism is the underdiscussed middle child of *isms*. Chinese uses a delightful phrase that translates to "There are words in your words" when the listener can tell a person is trying to say something without exactly saying it. In my circles, people don't talk about classism by name, but I hear it in their words. I've heard many statements from people that are subtly—or overtly—classist and spoken without a batted eye. James's discussion of favoritism touches on class as well:

> My brothers, show no partiality as you hold the faith in our Lord Jesus Christ, the Lord of glory. For if a man wearing a gold ring and fine clothing comes into your assembly, and a poor man in shabby clothing also comes in, and if you pay attention to the one who wears the fine clothing and say, "You sit here in a good place," while you say to

the poor man, "You stand over there," or, "Sit down at my feet," have you not then made distinctions among yourselves and become judges with evil thoughts? Listen, my beloved brothers, has not God chosen those who are poor in the world to be rich in faith and heirs of the kingdom, which he has promised to those who love him? But you have dishonored the poor man (James 2:1-6).

James doesn't mince words here. To show partiality is to harbor evil thoughts.

Favoritism will latch on to any difference to favor so long as it allows its host to gain or maintain a sense of superiority. In the Roman world, one's clothing provided the clearest insight into one's social status. In his commentary on the book of James, Roman social historian David Nystrom writes, "The issue is the uneven quality of the treatment, especially since it falls along the same status lines as was current in Roman culture. The word for 'insulted' is derived from *atimao*, a term used for oppressing the poor in the [Greek version of the Old Testament]."[2] According to this, dishonoring the poor is a form of oppression. Put another way, we oppress the poor when we treat the rich better for no other reason than that they are rich. When the church operates along the same status lines of the world, it is not reflective of that better country to come for which we wait, but of the darkness-powered world that is passing away.

James goes on later in the passage to be even harsher, branding those who show favoritism as transgressors of the great commandment to "love your neighbor as yourself" (James 2:8-9). Favoritism—what we often call *bias*—is a serious offense and one that will come under judgment in the end. "So speak and so act as those who are to be judged under the law of liberty" (James 2:12).

Right Sight and Itched Ears

Letting our natural tendencies rather than God's will dictate our actions leads to disordered living. The book of Judges shows the decline of Israel as they transitioned from rule by judge to eventual rule by kings. Throughout Judges, we read the refrain that *"everyone did what was right in his own eyes."* This was a diagnosis, not a compliment. God was not pleased. Israel was unwell. Each person decided for themselves how they would live, indulging their every preference and passion, and in this "anything goes" environment, corruption reigned.

We are not just bent on viewing ourselves and our actions in the best possible light, but also on hearing only what flatters us and reinforces our sense of self-righteousness. Second Timothy 4:3-4 speaks about what happens when this phenomenon infects the church. Itching ears lead to an abandonment of truth and turn toward falsehood that allows individuals to privilege their personal interests: "For the time is coming when people will not endure sound teaching, but having itching ears they will accumulate for themselves teachers to suit their own passions, and will turn away from listening to truth and wander off into myths." That time is here.

It's our nature to find people who will tell us what we know we will agree with; to seek out those who will not challenge the way we think or live. We choose our teachers in this way, but we don't stop there—we also seek to surround ourselves with entire communities of people who will leave us as we are, content in our own ways. Outsiders who challenge this status quo are a means of grace to help us see properly.

Putting the Gift to Work

If the ability to see is a gift we've been given to bless the church, then we owe it to others to use it. Luke 12:48 says, "Everyone to whom much was given, of him much will be required, and from him to whom they entrusted much, they will demand the more." What might change if we began to think of our ability to see the inside as part of the "much" we were given? Wouldn't those who lack bias, lack emotional connection, and have the benefit of distance owe it to others in their circle to gently help them see where their understanding is flawed or needs expanding? As an example, organizations value the perspective of outsiders by bringing them in to diagnose aspects of company culture. It is actually a blessing for those receiving feedback to be told where they could improve.

Of course, the outsider might not be able to see the flaws of their own group with as much clarity, and this is where things get exciting. Nick has something to learn from Angela, and Angela has something to learn from Steven, who has something to learn from Marlene, who has something to learn from Bouangern, and so forth and so on. Everyone is someone else's outsider, provided the right circumstances and configuration of people. What's more, we're outsiders in different ways. We have so much we can learn from each other, and with the help of a commitment to mutual submission out of reverence to Christ, with the help of a spirit of tenderhearted compassion that leads us to soften wounding blows into gentle rebukes, this gift has the power to enrich us both individually and as a community.

We should all invite this.

Reinvigorated by Vision

Imagine once more that church I described above. This time, people understand that their concerns are just parts of a multitude of legitimate concerns within their church. Here is a sampling of just some of the ways that understanding might shape how the church body functions:

People take initiative to find out what each other's core concerns are, helping them gain a bird's-eye view of their church community.

Concerns that affect fewer people are discussed rather than dismissed. Thoughtful effort is made to arrive at an informed decision that makes the "fringe" feel they belong.

A variety of cultural references are used—even knowing the majority might miss some—to ensure that the same people aren't always left out.

Congregants understand that some of the questions they bring to the Bible are culturally motivated, and they raise them with humility and willingness to engage with a spectrum of biblically minded responses.

Sin is recognized and rebuked as sin; its severity is not determined by how acceptable or taboo culture has deemed it.

Diverse perspectives are sought before big decisions, and "representative" diversity is not the target. Instead, a leadership sufficiently diverse to address the needs of the parts of the body that seem weaker is the goal.

Rather than as threats that should be rejected outright, challenges to the status quo are viewed as opportunities to seek biblical wisdom that might welcome necessary change.

Leaders are transparent about their weaknesses and blind spots and arrive upon plans and decisions with the margins in mind rather than seeing them as an afterthought.

Reflection Questions

1. What are some things that you have been able to see more clearly from a distance? How did that clarity help you make decisions?

_____

_____

_____

_____

2. How open would you consider yourself to receiving feedback or correction from "outsiders"?

_____

_____

_____

_____

3. What are some barriers that might prevent someone from speaking up about things they see in you or in your church? How can you help mitigate some of those?

_____

_____

_____

_____

4. What are some barriers to hearing in your life? Barriers to seeing?

_____

_____

_____

_____

5. Do you feel like you're able to be objective when it comes to evaluating the strengths and shortcomings of yourself and of the community to which you belong?

_____

_____

_____

_____

6. How can we have our hearts regularly primed for hearing the kinds of things that might make us better?

_____

_____

_____

_____

7. In what ways could you build rhythms into your life or your church that allow for outside perspective?

_____

_____

_____

_____

3

PERSPECTIVE

Seeing from Your Experience

As it is, God arranged the members in the body, each one of them, as he chose. If all were a single member, where would the body be?

1 CORINTHIANS 12:18-19

I was introduced to Indian music—or what Indians call "music"—as part of my world music class my senior year of college. By then, I'd learned 13 instruments and taken several hundred hours of ear training classes. I thought I knew all the notes that could be heard. Then came *ragas*, and suddenly, all these notes I didn't have names for and couldn't even hear properly reverberated with meaning. Notes I had been trained to hear as out of tune fit perfectly within a different system. They, too, were musical.

Author and psychologist Lisa McKay recently wrote about what she's learned from raising a child with ADHD, dyslexia, and autism. She writes,

> Parenting Dominic has forced me to confront my own culture-bound assumptions around what is "normal" and

how so much of what we call "disability" is contextually defined. After watching Dominic operate in villages in Vanuatu, I strongly suspect that if he had been born into a First Nations community in Australia or North America a couple of hundred years ago, he would have been hailed as a skilled and fearless hunter rather than labeled "disabled." But he wasn't. He was born to me and Mike. To this time. To this culture.[1]

Both our awareness of the existence of difference and our proximity to it change how we think about what we call "normal." Just as there are more ways to be musical than I thought, there are more ways to be human. Whether we realize it or not, we view the world through a lens particular to the cultural norms we live within.

Outsiders have the ability to identify truths about insiders that are only observable from a distance, but this isn't their only gift. They also bring a different perspective. What they are sensitive to, passionate about, and consider possible is shaped by their experiences. There are ways that either cultural distance from or similarity to the times and people of the Bible make Scripture either easier or more difficult to interpret and apply. Our presuppositions and assumptions are culturally informed. But whether its message seems close or distant, we should approach God's word humbly. Humility is also needed as we engage with those whose understanding of the Bible has been shaped by other cultural influences, knowing that ours has been too.

Who Benefits from Perspective?

I often see people frame diversity initiatives as being of primary benefit to the underrepresented party. But gaining new perspectives benefits both parties, and in many cases, the majority group is the greater beneficiary—largely because their relative lack of exposure means they have more to learn.

Not only do diverse perspectives ultimately benefit everyone, but the benefits are manifold. Different perspectives expose us to a wider array of existing realities and expand our collective imagination. Fewer people get overlooked and fewer options are left unconsidered when a variety of stakeholders are included in discussions about discipleship, church policies, programs, and culture. Diversity also enriches the pool of gifts available to put toward strengthening both the church as a whole and its individual members. In his commentary on 1 Corinthians, Thiselton writes, "Christians need *all* the resources of God's gifts that are spread throughout the church, and encountered through different individuals and in different forms."[2] Simply put, to counter the pull toward insularity and narrow-mindedness, we need each other's perspectives.

In recent years, I've had the opportunity to learn from a perspective often lacking in my church context: older women. Both my Korean private tutor and Korean language exchange partner are women about 15 years older than me, both Christian, and both living as expats—one in Hong Kong and one in France. When we speak, faith often comes up. I have, without a doubt, benefited from hearing them talk about God's faithfulness to them and what it means to them to be faithful to God. Through talking with them, I've become aware of some aspects of Christianity that are culturally derived. Multi-ethnic church pastor Mark DeYmaz writes,

> The fact is, much of what passes for religious doctrine or practical theology in our churches today is personal, preferential, or culturally bound. With this in mind, multi-ethnic church leaders must be able to recognize the differences. The ability to accommodate various forms of evangelical faith and worship without compromising doctrinal beliefs is an essential characteristic of those who would successfully brew ethnic blends. To do so, we must recognize that our way is only *a* way and not necessarily *the* way (in terms of right or wrong) to view or to do something in a church filled with people who are not like us.[3]

I'm not arguing for relativism or the idea that God is whoever we make him out to be, but maybe there's a reason narrative makes up so much of the Bible. Witnessing what God has done for his people is one of the most compelling ways we can learn about who God is and what he can do. There are facets of God we only glimpse in community; the more varied the community, the more multidimensional the image. Wheelchair user and Shakespeare lecturer Amy Kenny writes in *My Body Is Not a Prayer Request,* "There is a lot that limping has taught me over the years. Using my cane and wheelchair has given me a different perspective on who I am and who God is."[4] Her perspective is a needed gift to the church. We will never be able to get enough people together in a room that we can see God fully. But the more people we invite into the room, the more fully we can see him. God's identity is illuminated in different ways as his faithful followers meet him in the narratives of their lives and share how he's shown himself faithful to them. We uncover new facets of his goodness through the lives of others. We add one more name and tale to the ever-growing cloud of witnesses that bolster our knowledge of and trust in him.

New perspectives generate different questions and applications of Scripture. In chapter two, when describing the church of the insider, I mentioned that insiders think the most important questions the Bible answers are the ones they ask. Part of my interest in Christianity in other countries is curiosity about the kinds of questions Christians there might be asking. Think about it: After faith expanded to Gentiles at Pentecost, the church began to grapple with different questions about what it meant to be faithful to God. Issues such as food sacrificed to idols—issues that hadn't previously been raised because of the church's makeup—were now the content of Paul's letters.

During the pandemic, I was fascinated to watch the church take up new lines of inquiry about the application of Scripture. Suddenly, we were asking new questions about in-person meetings versus virtual meetings, grappling with ways we could continue fellowship when our old ways were not possible or permitted. These were new questions to most of us, but people on the margins of our communities had raised them earlier. Had more of our churches thought about this issue earlier in terms of members who have chronic illnesses or other barriers to joining in person, we would have asked these questions long ago. Instead of being caught off guard by a sudden change that impacted everyone, we would have benefited from considering and accommodating a perspective that has existed in the church all along.

Many Parted

Corinth was a preeminent city of the Roman Empire. Theologians Roy Ciampa and Brian Rosner explain, "Roman Corinth was prosperous, cosmopolitan, and religiously pluralistic…and obsessed with status, self-promotion, and personal rights."[5] To a culture preoccupied with self, Paul poses a fruitful question when he asks: "If all were a single member, where would the body be?" (1 Corinthians 12:19). The status-indifferent, self-abasing, rights-relinquishing approach to community he was proposing cut across the grain of a culture that saw difference only as something to exploit for personal gain. Paul urged Corinthian Christians to humbly consider the role of others as vital in the life of the church.

Our differences are not automatically our strength. If they were, why ever would we need grace? In fact, each new dimension of difference introduced into a group is an opportunity for factions and schisms to arise. This is human nature, and we have only our flesh to thank for this. But this is also why rich, multidimensional diversity is such a great opportunity to demonstrate the power of God. True unity moves from a far-flung ideal to a deepening reality when—through God's grace and despite our natural inclination—we endeavor toward humility and mutual submission out of reverence for Christ by the power of the Holy Spirit. The allure of Christ is clarified before an onlooking world, and reverence for him is understood to motivate individuals to live beyond themselves. When we are many parted yet one, we have only our Lord to thank for this.

Paul reminds us that the body is supposed to have many parts, and those parts all have something to contribute. Not just that, but the parts are *arranged*. Intention lies behind their design. God chose to give gifts to all, in the degree and configuration he desired, for the good of the whole. Just as exquisitely arranged as plants in a forest, stars in the sky, and cells in the body are our gifts and unique contributions. Our experiences are entrusted to us for the same reason God entrusts us with anything: to glorify him and build up his church. First Peter 4:10 says, "Each of you should use whatever gift you have received to serve others, as faithful stewards of God's grace in its various forms" (NIV). Insights into how to better love God or neighbors are forms of grace we must steward faithfully.

Keeping our perspectives to ourselves out of fear, shame, discomfort, or a sense of inferiority assumes that God made a mistake, that he isn't sovereign, or perhaps that he's just indifferent to how we were made or the things we've seen due to the times and places he's chosen for us to live. If we view our perspectives as resources to steward, our silence deprives our communities and buries our gifts. I'm sometimes tempted to keep what I believe to be important but potentially unpopular opinions to myself—especially when they go against something a leader has said—because I don't want to be "that person" or rock the boat. But ultimately, I am not burdening my community with these insights. Sharing them is an act of service. Your experiences are part of the package that enables you to edify your brother and sister in Christ in unique ways.

Of course, wisdom is needed when sharing these insights. Often, needed perspective erupts suddenly and thoughtlessly, rising from the frustration of being mistreated or the desire to clear one's chest. We may claim we're sharing to edify when we are actually sharing to shame or inflict harm. While we are not responsible for how our words are received, we are responsible for how they are delivered. We should weigh our words carefully. Gifts can be easily co-opted to serve ourselves rather than to serve others.

If All Were a Single Member

I don't want to just parrot the same "Diversity, Equity, and Inclusion" talking points that the world gives in defense of diversity. For the

Christian, capturing, considering, and honoring varied perspectives is about more than efficiency, power sharing, and increased objectivism—while those things may be true and good. It must also be more than a fad, though so often it feels like one. What *if* the whole body were a single member? What would we lose if we didn't have lips? How would we walk if all our toes were the same size? How would we be limited if our legs were merely another set of arms? And how does all of this play into God's glory?

We cannot function at our best without each other. We are each finite beings. Our wisdom, understanding, and resources are limited. Without different perspectives, churches run the risk of being mere echo chambers where people's ideas are reinforced and unchallenged by their community, and everyone thinks the same. Because of their experiences, outsiders possess a special perspective. Perhaps it's because they've seen a broader range of lived realities that exist—both their own as well as those of the majorities they've been exposed to—that they can see issues from multiple angles; they have an informed understanding of life on the inside as well as firsthand knowledge of life on the outside. Their perspective can challenge dominant thinking and broaden the options worth considering.

It's been said, "In essentials, unity; in nonessentials, liberty; in all things, charity." By having a church that allows for many members, I'm not talking about having lax or fluid theological commitments. I've seen my share of frustrated congregants leave churches they were never truly theologically aligned with in the first place because of the tension between their own beliefs and the church's core doctrine. But there are issues over which people can disagree charitably, where there is room to explore different applications of Scripture, or when the issue being considered isn't theological so much as cultural. Two churches with the same stated theological convictions can have drastically different cultures.

With the tenor of society today, most don't want to believe that *their* group could be the echo chamber; meanwhile, others don't even see echo chambers as innately bad. Each group claims exclusive possession of truth. But there are instances when the introduction of other perspectives doesn't signify the much-feared theological drift.

One of the reasons why it's good for the church to consist of many different people worshiping together is to help ensure that policies are more thoughtfully developed. You ask: *How does this or that policy work with the full range of people it could potentially affect?* By allowing people to share their perspectives, you end up with services and programs that are richer and have wider reach with fewer people left out.

For example, having someone who is unmarried be a part of the small group planning team might result in some small groups being held at a time or in a location that is more convenient for unmarried people than what was offered before. In that way, the majority group—married members with families—don't end up creating something that only works for them. Similarly, having someone of a lower literacy level be a part of helping to plan liturgy can help ensure that even those with lower reading ability can participate in those parts of the service. Or when you're looking for a new building or planning a new building project, including people who have accessibility issues on the planning committee can help the church find a building that works for the entire congregation. I know at our church, we have a ministry where we feed members from the community directly around the church who are of lower income levels. Having someone on that team who belongs to that demographic has been hugely helpful in brainstorming and planning the best ways to do outreach.

Over time, as you listen to your people, the "range" of groups under consideration grows. You develop a more nuanced awareness of the ways in which we differ from each other, and you recognize more fully how these differences shape others' unique needs and concerns.

Valuing Opportunities for Correction

Introducing outsiders into a new environment and giving them a voice is not just an act of kindness toward them, but a humble recognition that knowledge and wisdom exist outside ourselves and our tribe. We are just a facet of God's creation, not the focus of it. We are not the full expression of Christ's body on our own. Remembering that other individuals and groups have unique roles in God's kingdom is ultimately a comfort; fundamentally, it is an act of kindness toward ourselves.

Diverse perspectives also provide us with opportunities to see our flaws and the ways we fail to live out the vision of community that comes with citizenship in God's kingdom. This is grace! For my job, I review applications for a fellowship to ensure they are completed accurately so they can then be reviewed for merit. Occasionally, I must inform applicants that part of their application needs to be revised or properly completed before it can be considered. Every time, the response I get from them is one of pure gratitude because they recognize the value and honor of the award and appreciate the opportunity to fix an error they wouldn't have noticed on their own.

If we truly prized the opportunity to be refined and made like Christ, and if we truly recognized sanctification for the honor it is, we would be scavengers for whatever would help us achieve that. We would view correction as an aid to our one great pursuit. When our disordered love, honor, and consideration for our neighbor is brought to light and genuine love is our aim, we have been dealt a great mercy. When we are made aware of our need to repent—regardless of the smoothness of the rebuke—we are rerouted toward the path of life; we are provided with new encounters of grace. When our thinking is challenged to align more closely with God's design, we have been done a favor.

Research into diversity in the corporate sector may help us understand how it could benefit the church. *Harvard Business Review* reports,

> Diverse teams are more likely to constantly reexamine facts and remain objective. They may also encourage greater scrutiny of each member's actions, keeping their joint cognitive resources sharp and vigilant. By breaking up workplace homogeneity, you can allow your employees to become more aware of their own potential biases—entrenched ways

of thinking that can otherwise blind them to key information and even lead them to make errors in decision-making processes.[6]

I don't want to just parrot corporate talking points about how diversity leads to a stronger bottom line. For Christians, the best argument for why different perspectives should be welcomed is because that's God's design for the good of his body.

Having a different perspective can make you appreciate things others take for granted. When I lived in China, we gathered weekly to worship together with Christian students in an apartment rented and used exclusively for this purpose. For security reasons, not everyone was permitted to sing each week. We took turns. Even when it was your week to sing, you could do so only at a very low volume level. The last thing we wanted was to draw unwanted attention to ourselves. Almost two decades later, hardly a week goes by when I am in corporate worship and do not think about how amazing it is that we can gather freely without fear of being detained or shut down. I sometimes just close my eyes and stop singing and let the sound wash over me, grateful for our freedom. I gained a fresh appreciation for something that people who have only known this kind of worship experience take for granted.

The sensitivities, passions, and perspectives of outsiders enrich the whole. With loving forethought, God has arranged us as *he* saw fit, so our pursuit of flourishing diversity is foremost for *his* glory. The path toward God's vision for his kingdom is beset with obstacles, but in Christ, not one cannot be overcome. Seeing the beauty of each member's contribution requires humility and openness on the part of the insider and courage and trust on the part of the outsider. Both call for the wisdom and power of Christ.

Reflection Questions

1. Take one day this week to be mindful of the way different parts of your body support each other—how your nose helps your mouth, how your eyes help your ears, and how your hands help your feet. What other ways does your body work together? How does that help you understand the verse at the start of this chapter?

   _____

   _____

   _____

   _____

2. How likely are you to hold back from sharing your opinion because it may differ from others? How might you practice sharing your perspective in a Christlike way? In what situations would your voice provide valuable input and diversity to a group's mindset?

   _____

   _____

   _____

   _____

3. How do you normally respond to correction? What is your reaction when you're met with perspectives that are different from yours?

   _____

   _____

   _____

   _____

4. What does it look like to accept correction with humility? What do you think prevents this, both in yourself and in others? How can our identity in Christ act as a cushion and source of encouragement when we receive correction?

    _____

    _____

    _____

    _____

5. What does it look like to give correction with humility? In what ways have you struggled to do this in the past? How can our identity in Christ allow us to give correction more graciously?

    _____

    _____

    _____

    _____

6. What parts of the body of Christ are you most likely to dismiss as less valuable or more dispensable? What parts do you think may have come to the minds of Paul's original audience? How are those groups the same? How are they different?

    _____

    _____

    _____

    _____

4

EMPATHY
Seeing Others' Pain

You know the heart of a stranger,
because you were strangers.

EXODUS 23:9 (NKJV)

"I felt very angry this afternoon," Lily announced. "My Childcare group was at the play area, and we had a visiting group of Sevens, and they didn't obey the rules at *all*. One of them—a male; I don't know his name—kept going right to the front of the line for the slide, even though the rest of us were all waiting. I felt so angry at him. I made my hand into a fist, like this." She held up a clenched fist and the rest of the family smiled at her small defiant gesture.

"Why do you think the visitors didn't obey the rules?" Mother asked.

Lily considered, and shook her head. "I don't know. They acted like...like..."

"Animals?" Jonas suggested. He laughed.

"That's right," Lily said, laughing too. "Like animals." Neither child knew what the word meant, exactly, but it was often used to describe someone uneducated or clumsy, someone who didn't fit in.

"Where were the visitors from?" Father asked. Lily frowned, trying to remember. "Our leader told us, when he made the welcome speech, but I can't remember. I guess I wasn't paying attention. It was from another community. They had to leave very early, and they had their midday meal on the bus."

Mother nodded. "Do you think it's possible that their rules may be different? And so they simply didn't know what your play area rules were?"

Lily shrugged, and nodded. "I suppose."

"You've visited other communities, haven't you?" Jonas asked. "My group has, often."

Lily nodded again. "When we were Sixes, we went and shared a whole school day with a group of Sixes in their community."

"How did you feel when you were there?"

Lily frowned. "I felt strange. Because their methods were different. They were learning usages that my group hadn't learned yet, so we felt stupid."

Father was listening with interest. "I'm thinking, Lily," he said, "about the boy who didn't obey the rules today. Do you think it's possible that he felt strange and stupid, being in a new place with rules that he didn't know about?"

Lily pondered that. "Yes," she said, finally.

"I feel a little sorry for him," Jonas said, "even though I don't even know him. I feel sorry for anyone who is in a place where he feels strange and stupid."[1]

This scene from Lois Lowry's *The Giver* perfectly demonstrates how far a little self-reflection can go. Lily goes from wielding an angry fist at someone who, by her standards, didn't fit in, to understanding that person's perspective—prodded only by a simple question: "Haven't you?"

God asks us this question too. Time and again throughout Scripture, God asks his people, "Haven't you?" as he calls them to care for others who don't fit in—or rather, others who fit in differently. The call for Israel to remember its past frequently appears in tandem with laws prohibiting the mistreatment of others. It is also woven throughout the institution of the feasts such as Passover, Feast of Weeks, and Sukkoth, all of which contained some provision to look out for the less fortunate.

In Deuteronomy 24, when general laws were given, "You shall remember that you were a slave in Egypt" is repeated twice within five verses. But these reminders aren't so they will treat those currently enslaved better. No, they are so they will do good to the sojourner, the fatherless, and the widow (Deuteronomy 24:17-22). Even though the circumstances are not identical, the need arising from them is the same: divine intervention. Mention of Israel's past in Egypt was intended to propel them to graciousness. Hadn't Israel also been reliant on grace? Hadn't they been unable to change their circumstances? Hadn't they been vulnerable to mistreatment? Hadn't they felt helpless? Hadn't they, in their desperation, been seen by God?

Their history—when remembered—had the *potential* to keep them from perverting justice, from mistreating the vulnerable, from letting the helpless flounder, from overlooking the desperate. Whether it *did* or not is another story.

Recognizing Opportunities for Empathy

We've looked at the vision outsiders have of the inside and the value of their unique perspective—in terms of their outlook on the world and faith, as well as on the wider church. In addition to seeing the inside and having an ability to see from the vantage point of their unique experiences, the outsider's gifts of sight are also specifically a gift to other outsiders—but to put this gift to use, we must use our time on the outside as an invitation to empathize with the mistreatment of others.

In the New Testament parable of the unmerciful servant, we see a similar principle at play. A man straining under the burden of enormous debt is shown mercy by his master and his debts are forgiven. Yet when this forgiven debtor is approached by a man needing mercy for the small amount of money he owes, the first debtor puts the other man in prison. The forgiven man's master asks him the pivotal question: *Haven't you?* "I forgave you all that debt because you pleaded with me. And should not you have had mercy on your fellow servant, as I had mercy on you?" (Matthew 18:32-33). Hadn't this servant been a debtor shown mercy? Hadn't he also been unable to pay? Hadn't he felt desperate and, in his desperation, been relieved by his master?

People often go through similar experiences yet never stop to think about how their experience relates to others. Or they encounter others, as Lily did in *The Giver*, but fail to recall when they stood in those people's shoes.

A Spoonful of Self-Reflection

Several years ago, many of my close friends found themselves somewhere I could tell they'd rarely, if ever, been before: on the unflattering side of a statistic. Previously, these friends had either been seen as individuals or belonged to part of a group that statistics represented positively; they didn't have to worry about being regularly seen through the lens of negative statistics or distrust. For the first time, they were burdened by questions like, "Will I have to convince these people I'm meeting for the first time that I'm one of the good ones? Or that I'm more than I appear?" But this reversal of fortunes was ironic; these same people who now desperately wanted separation from unsavory statistics had been all too content to use these numbers to assess others.

I watched as these friends went from being proud of all that was associated with them to rushing to set themselves apart from those who were definitely not like them. They exhibited a previously undemonstrated ability to speak for those potentially misrepresented by statistics that now included themselves. Suddenly, there were all manner of reasons why the numbers had come out as they had, and—as they were eager to point out—they were some of "the good ones." "Nuance!" they demanded. "See me for who I am!" they urged. "Understand those people's situations!" they pleaded. *Before*, statistics gave them a useful overview of what they needed to know about people. *Now*, statistics were something to parse alongside personal stories, justifications, and a list of caveats longer than a CVS receipt.

I watched, fascinated. I'd felt and expressed everything they had when facing overly simplified and unflattering statistics that did not allow me to be seen as the individual I was. These friends were doing something I'd been doing my whole life: advocating to be seen for who they were rather than be lumped together with their worst statistics. What I knew as a phenomenon common to so many misunderstood or misrepresented outsiders was, for the first time, showing itself in these peers who had enjoyed most of life on the inside. Many thought this feeling was unique to their experience; in their eyes, surely no statistic had ever so failed to tell the full story as this one.

Outsiders understand all too well this impulse to fight back against being painted with an overly broad brush. The same impulse behind every *#NotAll[_____]* reflex stirs their hearts with the longing for the world to recognize that numbers don't tell the complete story. As I watched my friends navigate this feeling for the first time, I wished so badly they'd pause to reflect on their emotional responses. I hoped they'd stop and wonder about others before them who'd faced misrepresentation, about how those groups who'd been reduced to statistics had responded to similar entreaties for nuance in the past. I prayed they'd see those groups as the same story-bearers they were and attempt to understand each of their individual complexities.

This happens on a more global scale as well. Once in graduate school, I was researching Chinese nationalism at the turn of the twentieth century. *Uncle Tom's Cabin* had been translated into Chinese and enjoyed wide popularity. In the introduction, the translator—a Chinese man— had drawn parallels between the experience of African slaves in America and China's very recent past. Having just gone through their own war with Western countries and been on the receiving end of oppression and mistreatment, China should have been sympathetic to the Black experience, right? Hadn't they also been taken advantage of and seen as inferior? Yet soon thereafter, I came across Kang Youwei, a much-admired Chinese intellectual, in a book about the construction of racial identities in China and Japan written by Dutch historian of modern China, Frank Dikötter. Dikötter writes,

> Kang Youwei, one of the most acclaimed philosophers of the late nineteenth century, judged that Africans, 'with their iron faces, silver teeth, slanting jaws like a pig, front view like an ox, full breasts and long hair, their hands and feet dark black, stupid like sheep or swine', should be whitened by intermarriage, although he feared that no refined white girl would ever agree to mate with a 'monstrously ugly black'. 'Whites' and 'yellows' who married 'blacks' as a contribution to the purification of mankind should therefore be awarded a medal with the inscription 'Improver of the race', whereas 'browns or blacks whose characteristics are too bad, whose physical appearance is too ugly or who carry a disease should be given a sterilizing medication to stop the perpetuation of their race.'[2]

The solidarity we might expect is nowhere to be seen.

One thing I've realized is that the fainter or less frequent one's sense of being on the outside, the more likely this gift goes unused or even undetected. I so often see others processing situations the same way another outsider would and then very excitedly think, *Slow down and sit in that feeling for a while.* This ability to empathize with others, to ask yourself, "Haven't you?" and then extend a little more patience and grace, is a gift we must recognize and put to use.

Is Empathy Actually Good?

In recent years, empathy has come under fire. Even a quick internet search reveals quite a large body of recent articles exposing the allegedly "ugly downside" to empathy. In fact, Yale psychologist Paul Bloom has concluded that, perhaps surprisingly, empathy does *not* lead to more moral decision making:

> When we rely on empathy to make moral decisions, [Bloom] says, we end up prioritizing the person whose suffering we can easily relate to over that of any number of others who seem more distant. Indeed, studies have shown that empathy does encourage irrational moral decisions that favor one individual over the masses...Empathy zooms us in on the attractive, on the young, on people of the same race. It zooms us in on the one rather than the many. And so it distorts our priorities.[3]

But for the outsider, it doesn't have to be this way. Empathizing with those who aren't young or who are culturally seen as less attractive or worthy may very well come easier for us because we, almost by definition, are the ones culture sees as less worthy.

Another accusation lobbied against empathy is that it focuses on feelings of the sufferer rather than truth. To be clear, we can feel badly for those who are suffering the consequences of their sin while still being committed to truth and their highest good. It is possible to do both. Grace and truth take wisdom and discernment to balance, but having empathy needn't mean dispensing with accountability or correction. In fact, outsiders who are deeply aware of the ways they've struggled with unintentional or intractable sins would be better able to empathize with others experiencing the same. A recognition of our sin is not just valuable before God but makes us better neighbors too.

Letting Transfer Empower Empathy

My favorite class as an undergraduate student was educational psychology. Among the cognitive skills covered, the concept of "transfer of knowledge"—appropriately applying the lessons you learned from one situation to another—was both the most fascinating and one of the most important. Teaching for transfer was a central goal, and students who knew when and how to do this were well-poised to succeed across a variety of fields.

Transfer types vary. "Negative transfer" occurs when you misapply previous learning to a new situation, while "positive transfer" enhances your performance in new contexts. "Far transfer" enables you to use past knowledge to leap between remote contexts and "high road transfer" is the "deliberate effortful abstraction and a search for connections."[4] When faced with two situations that are not identical, this means thinking carefully through what appropriate domains of commonality might exist beneath the surface between the two.

For example, with a little reflection, being an outsider in one area can prime the pump for understanding others who are outsiders in different ways. Earlier last year, when asking a friend her opinion about the benefits of being single, she wrote, "As a teacher, being single has helped me better relate to the experience of neurodivergent students. They navigate a world and school system that was not designed for them. I navigate a world designed for couples and coupled people." She transferred the lessons she'd learned from being an outsider from one group—being single—to better engage with those who lived as outsiders from a different group. On the surface, singleness and neurodivergence may seem unrelated, but abstracting out to the accessibility of support systems for each allowed this friend to find a connection.

We cannot consider ourselves above being patient with those who are slow to learn because we can find no example of that in the life and love of Jesus. While our otherness has perhaps primed us more easily for empathy, exercising that empathy is what makes this perspective a gift. We are stewards of everything that gift endows—and from those to whom much is given, much is required. Let us be instruments of grace.

A World Without Empathy

One of the alternatives to empathy is moral rationalism: the belief that we can and should rely on our rational selves to make decisions. If we lived in a world where we were always able to perceive others without the blinders of our biases and take others at their word when they shared their hurt with us, moral rationalism could be acceptable—but this isn't the world we live in. Besides this, having a rational understanding of something is far less comforting to the person in pain. "You wouldn't understand" is a frequent complaint in arguments, and empathetic understanding often leads to better outcomes. There's greater urgency to solve issues when we've felt the pain.

There's a scene in a TV show I like where the male and female lead characters switch body sensations. The woman is a bodyguard and is frequently on the receiving end of a lot of fists. Every time she gets hit, the man feels it and curses her silently from his home. Some weeks later, he is immobilized and feels like he's dying. The culprit? Period cramps. "How do women work through this every month?!" he asks incredulously. As the owner of his company, he immediately instates period leave for all female employees.

Shortly after moving to DC, I became a small group leader at my church. My coleader, Tim, spoke with a stutter. He had also been homeschooled and came from a very conservative family background. Based on his profile alone, I would likely assume certain things about him. But the better I got to know him, the more I came to realize that his stuttering had made him able to relate to some of the specific struggles Black people encounter in spaces where we are the minority.

As our friendship grew, I began to investigate speech disorders more. I watched movies and read articles on the topic, and I asked him questions about his experience. I found he was also able to understand a little bit of what it was like for me as a Black woman. Because he recognized that I might be tempted—as a Black woman leader in a majority-white church—to work overtime so I could prove myself and my leadership abilities to others, he once encouraged me to stop trying so hard. He assured me that I was enough—and that I could relax because I didn't have anything to prove. Let me tell you, that was *so* freeing! And it blew my mind that this specific insight came from a white guy. And yet, he was sensitive to this concern because he himself felt like he was constantly trying to disprove assumptions others might have of him based on how fluidly he was able to speak.

On one occasion, I took Tim to an event at Howard University for Black Christians where he was the only white guy in the room. Another time, he brought me to a holiday party for friends and family of people in his speech therapy group. This compassionate community allowed them to feel like they could speak at ease, without worrying about being rushed or making a bad first impression. Even though we were very different from each other and came from very different backgrounds, our experiences as outsiders helped us to serve and understand each other better. While he couldn't recognize my *exact* pain, his understanding of his *own* pain allowed him to identify the defense mechanisms we shared.

In a Humans of New York story, a Black man talked about the five minutes it takes him to settle into a space where he's the only Black person present:

> That's my challenge. To walk into a room, and not have to work mentally. To be aware of my blackness; to not forget it. But to also be present. And focused. And productive…I've had decades of practice, but it still takes me five minutes. To transition. To stop worrying if people believe that I belong here. To stop feeling like a unicorn. It's five minutes of work that nobody else in the room has to do.

Many responses to this post came from women working in male-dominated fields who felt his story resonated with them. One in particular struck me. A woman shared that she'd never had to think about her race until she moved overseas and lived abroad during 9/11. She explained that due to racial tension, her daily routines were disturbed for fear for her safety. She was relieved to finally return to the US so she wouldn't have to be a minority anymore, and then it hit her: "So many people will never in their life feel that 'relief' of going back to not having to think about it," she wrote. "That experience changed my whole way of thinking."[5]

The Empathy of Christ

We must recognize the ability to connect with others because we have shared in some aspect of their experience as a kingdom good. It is not the whole of the kingdom's goodness, but it is certainly a part. Jesus, our great High Priest, has set for us an amazing example of empathy. Hebrews 4:15 says, "For we do not have a high priest who is unable to sympathize with our weaknesses, but one who in every respect has been tempted as we are, yet without sin." It is a comfort and reassurance to know that he knows our experiences. Theologian Gareth Lee Cockerill explains that this is stronger than just a feeling: "This is a 'sympathy' that leads to active assistance."[6]

R. Kent Hughes illustrates the sympathy of Christ using two string instruments in the same room. The striking of one instrument produces a "sympathetic resonance" in the other. "Christ's instrument was just like ours in every way. And hear this! He took that instrument, that body, to Heaven with him. It is his priestly body. And when a chord is struck in the weakness of our human instrument, it resonates in his. There is no note of human experience that does not play on Christ's exalted human instrument."[7]

Each one of us has been commanded to carry one another's burdens: "Bear one another's burdens, and so fulfill the law of Christ" (Galatians 6:2). What often sets outsiders apart is their ability to identify unspoken burdens and better understand those vocalized. Part of why I gravitated toward Asian American churches my first few years back in the States after China was because being with other minorities allowed me to stop feeling like I had to defend or explain the truth of discrimination and its impact on me. My white friends might like to share this burden with me, but they often don't know how. Sometimes, even their desire to share these kinds of burdens multiplies them rather than lightening them, because in my moments of weakness, I don't want to assume the additional role of teacher. There is a certain respite that outsiders provide for each other in this way.

Empathy makes the church better because it enables us to mourn with those who mourn and rejoice with those who rejoice. Instead of wielding metaphorical fists at "problem" people without considering their perspective, we stop first to ask: Haven't I also been reliant on grace? Haven't I also faced battles where I was powerless to change my circumstances? Haven't I ever been vulnerable to mistreatment? Haven't I felt helpless? And in my desperation, haven't I been seen by God?

Empathy is also a gift to those who possess it. It conforms them more closely to the character of Christ. To advance and mature in sanctification is an end in itself. To share in the character of Christ is an honor and joy. To the extent that our empathy is untainted by proud assumptions, is rooted in humility, and is employed toward being more loving, gracious, and merciful, that is enough. Hearts are changed when a community is dedicated to approaching the experience of others with humility so that they might connect their experiences to those of others—even if it's never verbalized. A church full of people focused on extending compassion to their neighbors is a victory for the bride of Christ.

Reflection Questions

1. What role have you seen vulnerability play in building bridges
   of empathy? What different ways of showing vulnerability might
   lead to a more compassionate community?

   _____

   _____

   _____

   _____

2. When have you been the recipient of empathy? How did it impact
   you? Looking back on times when you navigated something difficult or painful, what did you receive—or wish you had received—
   from others who shared your experience?

   _____

   _____

   _____

   _____

3. How do you normally respond to someone telling you about something you haven't experienced yourself? What role does the practice
   of empathetic listening play in your reaction? If you feel Christ calling
   you to make changes to your approach, what might that look like?

   _____

   _____

   _____

   _____

4. Think about your experiences of feeling unsafe or insecure, or
   imagine what it would be like to have your greatest sources of
   security threatened. In what ways do you imagine that your emotional responses to these situations are universal? In what ways

might other individuals or groups with different backgrounds have a different response?

_____

_____

_____

_____

5. How might empathy improve your interpersonal relationships? How might a more widespread embrace of empathy change the way your church operates? How might it impact a newcomer's Sunday morning experience?

_____

_____

_____

_____

6. Whether it's your church, your workplace, or your neighborhood, what practical steps can you take to cultivate empathy within your community?

_____

_____

_____

_____

7. How does the example of Christ's incarnational ministry encourage you to change your approach to interacting with people who are different from you?

_____

_____

_____

_____

GIFTS OF DEPENDENCE

Outsiders can teach us about our limits and our need to depend on each other and God. The following chapters look at these gifts of dependence and interdependence.

5

LACK AND LIMITS

A Grace-Filled Awareness of Need

Beware lest you say in your heart, "My power and the might of my hand have gotten me this wealth." You shall remember the LORD your God, for it is he who gives you power to get wealth, that he may confirm his covenant that he swore to your fathers, as it is this day.

DEUTERONOMY 8:17-18

Sometimes we find ourselves on the outside not because of who we are, but because of what we lack. (Repeat after me: "Who we are is not what we do or do not have!") We were made to depend on God and on each other, but self-sufficiency—so highly prized by our culture—often threatens this. Contrary to our design, we associate needing help with feeling shame; instead of guiding us to God, limited resources propel us to self-pity or pretense. Yet those who have known scarcity and met God in its midst become rich, regardless of an increase in their material resources. Those whose bodies give frequent reminders of human frailty and finitude don't live under the deception of endless days or energy—and often their hearts are more receptive to humankind's call to community.

Called to Depend

God wants us to seek him to meet our needs. When we neglect to come to him and turn instead to lesser things, he is displeased—meanwhile, our efforts to circumvent him are fruitless, because only God provides true sustenance. As the giver of life, he wants us to find it in him. As the God of all comfort, he wants us to take solace in him. As the provider of peace that transcends understanding, he wants us to trade our restlessness and unease for his clarity and confidence. God tirelessly says, "Come," so that he may meet all our needs "according to his riches in glory in Christ Jesus" (Philippians 4:19). He longs to be leaned on.

We are not needy by mistake; we are needy by nature. But we would rather hide this aspect of ourselves from God and from each other. Perhaps the openly needy people we know are seen as a drag by their communities. When I experienced a season of neediness, I confessed to a friend that I didn't want to ask my church for help because I didn't want to be the Black woman with her hand out at the church filled with white conservatives. This fear of being needy wasn't irrational—I've observed the thinning patience of those once eager to help, heard the sighs at yet another request, watched generosity be leveraged as a tool for control. Owing people—whether in money or in deed—can weigh us down even more than the original need itself. Ed Welch in *Side by Side* writes, "It's not easy to ask for help. We spend a lot of time hiding our neediness because we are afraid of what people will think…For me, being needy is a sign of weakness, and, given a choice, I prefer to appear strong or at least competent."[1]

Especially in a culture where independence is next to godliness, dependence is failure. But today, the society we live in has been built on this belief, and it couldn't look further from the picture of the church that we see in Acts: "And they were selling their possessions and belongings and distributing the proceeds to all, as any had need" (Acts 2:45). We have forgotten how God often uses material lack and human limitations to remind us that he—our eternal, all-powerful Lord—is our greatest need.

Lack

Many of us go through life unaware of just how needy we are. We might acknowledge seasons of need that punctuate otherwise stable patterns of self-sufficiency, but often we justify them by making the distinction that this neediness is circumstantial and temporary. "Something bad happened," we might say later, once we believe we have returned to our default state of independence and control. "I just needed some help getting back on my feet."

With our emergency funds and access to healthcare and every other security middle-class Americans enjoy, our innate neediness is often out of mind. Our lives are stable. Tragedy is unthinkable. We feel we're invincible—but we're not, and though excess allows us to forget this truth, lack unmasks it. Though we may experience lack, it doesn't tell the whole story of who we are. We are not lacking because we lack. We are simply human; only God is self-sufficient. Lack reminds us of the disquieting truth that there is nothing in this world we can cling to that cannot be taken away.

Limits

In addition to denying our neediness when it comes to material possessions, we are also reluctant to share the other ways we might need help. Things like sickness, disease, and tragedy offer painful reminders of our limits. At a moment's notice, the ground beneath us can crumble away. Even small inconveniences remind us that the comfort, health, and happiness we often take for granted are gifts and not guarantees. How many times has a head cold given you renewed appreciation for the everyday blessing of being able to breathe through your nose?

When we face limits, asking for help can take courage, can force us to confront feelings of shame about needing help in the first place, and

can test what we really believe about our community and its purpose.
Author Lyndsey Medford put it perfectly,

> Sometimes asking for help feels like "failure" at indepen-
> dence…but it's actually succeeding at interdependence.
> What feels like vulnerability is actually experiencing com-
> munal strength and resilience. What feels like taking from
> others is actually giving them the gift of purpose, love, and
> community. Our needs are gifts that remind us that we
> belong together.[2]

For people who pride themselves on being independent, the leap
from exalting independence to embracing interdependence feels vast—
but being strengthened by community is beautiful. It is a kingdom
perk. We are a part of something greater than ourselves.

To me, two of the most powerful biblical examples of interdependence are Exodus 17's story about Moses's need to keep his hands lifted
during battle, and Luke 5's account of the paralytic whose friends lowered
him through the roof to see Jesus. In Exodus 17, Joshua is "voluntold" to
go fight Amalek while Moses, Aaron, and Hur keep watch:

> Moses, Aaron, and Hur went up to the top of the hill. When-
> ever Moses held up his hand, Israel prevailed, and whenever
> he lowered his hand, Amalek prevailed. But Moses' hands
> grew weary, so they took a stone and put it under him, and he
> sat on it, while Aaron and Hur held up his hands, one on one
> side, and the other on the other side. So his hands were steady
> until the going down of the sun. And Joshua overwhelmed
> Amalek and his people with the sword (Exodus 17:10-13).

I'm always moved by the image of Aaron and Hur providing lit-
eral, physical support to Moses. We can imagine Moses's fatigue, his
arms shaking as he prays that the decisive victory blow will be dealt so
he can finally lower them. Though God didn't provide him with this
immediate relief, he did provide Aaron and Hur to hold his hands
steady the whole day.

We see a similar interdependence illustrated much later in Luke 5, when a paralyzed man's friends help him seek healing from Jesus by lowering him through a roof: "And behold, some men were bringing on a bed a man who was paralyzed, and they were seeking to bring him in and lay him before Jesus, but finding no way to bring him in, because of the crowd, they went up on the roof and let him down with his bed through the tiles into the midst before Jesus" (Luke 5:18-19).

Both the paralytic man and Moses had reached their limits. Both found at their side in their time of need others who could assist them in some way, whether it was spending the day holding Moses's hands up or making a cot, scaling a roof then digging a hole through it, and lowering an adult male down to land before Jesus in a crowded room. This is what community is meant to be.

Knowing our limitations, God was kind to institute the Sabbath for his people as a day of rest. This was a departure from the seven-day workweek that also had financial implications. In *Christians in an Age of Wealth*, New Testament scholar Craig Blomberg writes,

> Their potential incomes were reduced by 1/7 as a result. God wanted his people to realize that making money was not the be-all and end-all of Life. Indeed, 3 of the 10 most Central Commandments given to ancient Israel were designed to protect them against the seduction of material possessions. Even more obviously than the Sabbath command, the injunctions against stealing and coveting one's neighbor's property recognize the perennial human temptation to want to amass for oneself the greatest amount of wealth possible by whatever means.[3]

But God didn't just give us the Sabbath; he gave us each other and still even to others a deeper awareness of what is true of us all. Amy Kenny writes, "Those of us who are disabled already know how to welcome interdependence as a habitual practice without demonizing our bodies in the process."[4] We can learn to live faithfully as we were designed, limits and all, from examples like this.

The heart behind God's law is to help us, his finite people, honor our limits. Included within this is being vulnerable enough to identify our limits, express them to others, and trust God for provision when they have been met. Seeking God's strength isn't something he intended us to save for worst-case scenarios—God doesn't just want to be sought in times of crisis when we're on the brink of collapse, but envisions us coming to him frequently, asking him for rest as well as making our needs known to the community.

I recently read an article in the *Washington Post* written by a person with a disability describing bootstrap culture: the idea that we can just work harder to achieve what we want and pull ourselves by ourselves out of whatever trouble we find ourselves in. He writes,

> All of this affects life in a disabled body—a body that is constantly observed and assigned both too much expectation and little whatsoever. This mixed messaging and over emphasis on personal independence has led me to poorly defined goals and confusion about what my value is. Growing up there was a lot of pressure for me to be as independent as possible but often little investment in my success. I felt judged every time I needed others or couldn't complete a task or goal. Worse, I grew nervous that no one really expected that much from me anyway. This dynamic isn't entirely unique to me. Disabled people are often told—by our families, peers, media, the world—that to be acceptable, we need to be exceptional. I push my body to its limits, constantly working to suppress my body's every need. As though the presence of needs and limitations aren't integral parts of being a human, disabled or no. But the message they sell us is a lie. There's no real benefit to going it alone. We all have limits. We all need others to get by.[5]

Sadly, this isn't the message we usually hear. Instead, we're taught to put faith in ourselves. "The ability to do it all lies deep within each one of us," we're told—but this is a lie! Jen Oshman exposes the Christian-coated worldly messages of self-reliance being peddled today for what they are. "This faith in self only makes sense for a certain population in a certain context," she writes in "Girl, Follow Jesus," her review of Rachel Hollis's *Girl, Stop Apologizing.* "How many people across history and across the globe can 'believe you're capable of making changes to become whatever kind of person you want to be'? It's a cruel joke to say to the disabled, to the poor, to the oppressed, 'you've got to decide right now that you can be whoever you want to be and achieve whatever you want to achieve.'"[6]

In the Sermon on the Mount in Matthew 5:3, Jesus says, "Blessed are the poor in spirit, for theirs is the kingdom of heaven." The New Living Translation presents this verse as, "God blesses those who are poor and realize their need for him, for the Kingdom of Heaven is theirs." Frequently, we find an overlap between those of modest means and those who are poor in spirit. While it comes with its share of serious and sometimes heartbreaking challenges, poverty ultimately provides better conditions for a poor spirit to grow.

The Dangers of Plenty

I was once given a tour of a museum under construction and was required to wear protective gear. Everyone who entered the premises had to protect themselves from the potential hazards within. The experience led me to reflect on how often we find ourselves luxuriating in the presumption of safety, helmets off, unaware that danger is even a possibility.

In Philippians 4:12, Paul talks about learning "how to abound." I hadn't given much thought to how peculiar it was that he would need to learn how to have abundance. Isn't abundance a walk in the park? Why would we even need help living in plenty? Isn't the struggle most intense in want? But the more I thought about it, the more I saw that plenty—crafty as it can be—comes with its own insidious traps.

First, we often do not recognize our plenty. We have what we need, and we even have a generous portion of things we simply want, yet ingratitude leads us to focus on what we lack. Oblivious to just how much we have, ungratefulness traps us in a mindset of scarcity and prevents us from recognizing our prosperity. Solomon pities such a man in Ecclesiastes 6:3: "If a man fathers a hundred children and lives many years, so that the days of his years are many, but his soul is not satisfied with life's good things, and he also has no burial, I say that a stillborn child is better off than he." The inability to be satisfied with what one has is anything but enviable.

We also perpetually raise the bar for what constitutes "plenty." The Diderot Effect is a social phenomenon related to consumption that posits first that people purchase in alignment with their sense of identity and second, that new purchases deviant to that lead to spiraling consumption. Denis Diderot, the French philosopher who wrote the essay, "Regrets on Parting with my Old Dressing Gown," describes receiving the gift of a beautiful new gown fancier than his other possessions. Over time, he grew dissatisfied with his other tawdry old things. Upgrading the rest of his possessions, from his chair and rug to paintings on the wall, he plunged himself into debt and lamented, "I was absolute master of my old dressing gown but I have become a slave to my new one…The poor man may take his ease without thinking of appearances, but the rich man is always under a strain…Fear the touch of wealth…Poverty has its freedoms; opulence has its obstacles." It's true that sometimes having more can make us less satisfied. Our possessions, whether material or immaterial (such as power, reputation, and relationships), provide limited and temporary potency. Our pleasures will have short shelf lives unless rooted in Jesus.

We also make light of materialism, perhaps because it is so pervasive or because it seems less serious. Jesus would say otherwise: "Do not lay up for yourselves treasures on earth, where moth and rust destroy and where thieves break in and steal, but lay up for yourselves treasures in heaven, where neither moth nor rust destroys and where thieves do not break in and steal. For where your treasure is, there your heart will be also" (Matthew 6:19-21). He reiterates this sentiment later: "As for what was sown among thorns, this is the one who hears the word, but the cares of the world and the deceitfulness of riches choke the word, and it proves unfruitful" (Matthew 13:22).

Powerfully convicting. Theologian Stanley Hauerwas writes, "It is hard to imagine any text more relevant to the situation of churches in the West. Why we are dying seems very simple. It is hard to be a disciple and be rich. Surely, we may think, it cannot be that simple, but Jesus certainly seems to think that it is that simple."[7]

Of all the things I can imagine someone being disciplined for in the church, I cannot imagine someone being called out for materialism, even by a friend. But some of the "church discipline" of the prophets does just that. Amos 6:4-7 says,

> Woe to those who lie on beds of ivory and stretch themselves out on their couches, and eat lambs from the flock and calves from the midst of the stall, who sing idle songs to the sound of the harp and like David invent for themselves instruments of music, who drink wine in bowls and anoint themselves with the finest oils, but are not grieved over the ruin of Joseph! Therefore they shall now be the first of those who go into exile, and the revelry of those who stretch themselves out shall pass away.

Jesus also offers words of warning in Luke 12:15, saying, "Take care, and be on your guard against all covetousness, for one's life does not consist in the abundance of his possessions." An entire chapter of Revelation is dedicated to the destruction of Babylon for her materialism: "As she glorified herself and lived in luxury, so give her a like measure of torment and mourning, since in her heart she says, 'I sit as a queen, I am no widow, and mourning I shall never see'" (Revelation 18:7).

Here are a few more examples:

> See the man who would not make God his refuge, but trusted in the abundance of his riches and sought refuge in his own destruction! But I am like a green olive tree in the

house of God. I trust in the steadfast love of God forever and ever (Psalm 52:7-8).

If riches increase, set not your heart on them (Psalm 62:10).

Whoever trusts in his riches will fall, but the righteous will flourish like a green leaf (Proverbs 11:28).

Keep your life free from love of money, and be content with what you have, for [God] has said, "I will never leave you nor forsake you" (Hebrews 13:5).

Those who desire to be rich fall into temptation, into a snare, into many senseless and harmful desires that plunge people into ruin and destruction. For the love of money is a root of all kinds of evils. It is through this craving that some have wandered away from the faith and pierced themselves with many pangs (1 Timothy 6:9-10).

Clearly, the dangers of wealth are both many and serious. Skipping the warning label on riches comes at a steep cost. New Testament Professor David Turner writes, "Greed and secular concerns are also effective in thwarting the reception of the Kingdom message, evidently when the demands of discipleship confront a materialistic lifestyle."[8] By our lifestyles and choices, we expose ourselves to both weakening and strengthening influences. The excess of materialism is a weakening influence. Possessions, while mostly seen as harmless by many, may actually prevent us from responding to the kingdom message as we should. Randy Alcorn writes in *Money, Possessions, and Eternity*, "The truth is, if our hearts were not captive to materialism, we would neither subsidize nor tolerate materialism in churches, nonprofit ministries, and for-profit businesses."[9]

I know what you're thinking: *I'm not materialistic. Those people who make more money than me are.* I have had the same thoughts, but I'll never forget the time my materialism smacked me in my face. During my first year in Laos, the house where I lived did not have a washer and dryer. I had saved up my laundry over the month and was headed to have my clothes washed by someone. I had just loaded my two bags of clothes into the back of a *tuk tuk* truck when I ran into a coworker. They asked, "Whose clothes are those?"

I answered, "Those are my clothes."

They were stunned. *"All of those clothes are your clothes?!"* My face went red. (It didn't really because I'm Black, but it totally would have if I wasn't!) Why *did* I have so many clothes to live in a place with one climate?

The last trap of plenty is our sense of self-sufficiency, slowly administering its poison like an IV drip. Israel herself had to prepare to move on from the land of want in the wilderness to the land of plenty in Canaan because God saw the traps that lay ahead. Deuteronomy 8:12-18 says,

> Lest, when you have eaten and are full and have built good houses and live in them, and when your herds and flocks multiply and your silver and gold is multiplied…then your heart be lifted up, and you forget the LORD your God, who brought you out of the land of Egypt, out of the house of slavery, who led you through the great and terrifying wilderness, with its fiery serpents and scorpions and thirsty ground where there was no water, who brought you water out of the flinty rock, who fed you in the wilderness with manna that your fathers did not know, that he might humble you and test you, to do you good in the end. Beware lest you say in your heart, "My power and the might of my hand have gotten me this wealth." You shall remember the LORD your God, for it is he who gives you power to get wealth, that he may confirm his covenant that he swore to your fathers, as it is this day.

As we read on, we see God warn them that this forgetfulness would lead to their perishing, not their ultimate flourishing.

I talked before about having a singular better boast. If ever one was needed, it is today. We live in an age of "My power and the might of my hand have gotten me this wealth." Just think about the people who talk about "my money" or what they've earned. People who ask, "Why should my hard-earned money go to someone who hasn't worked for it?" Wealth is touted as favor on Sunday, but the rest of the week, it's attributed to one's own efforts. Meanwhile, those of lesser means are seen as less worthy, a misbelief that tempts us to ask: "If God also gives them the power to get wealth, why haven't they?"

The Gift of Lack

During a season of scarcity and need after losing my job, eye- and heart-opening discomforts produced new people to empathize with and fresh awareness of my idols. I became far more aware of my relationship to money when I didn't have it than when I did. Money turned out to be one of those grains of sand under my house I mistook for a rock.

I will forever treasure the more immediate and deep ways I experienced God during that time. In James 2:5, he speaks of a paradox: "Has not God chosen those who are poor in the world to be rich in faith and heirs of the kingdom, which he has promised to those who love him?" But for lack, I might not otherwise have been so enriched.

Before finding a new permanent job, I prayed I would carry that spirit of dependence and faith into the land of plenty once that season was over. I was nervous that returning to comfort might mean a loss of intimacy and the good kind of neediness that God delights in when we know we aren't in control.

I couldn't help but wonder about the transition from desperate struggle and felt need to relative ease and stability. I also began to ponder if true financial stability wasn't found in savings and a stable income, but rather in having the right orientation toward money and material possessions—and in relying on the hand that provides both. What would become of my dependence on God when I was back to working the earth?

Lack simply provides better conditions for a poor spirit to grow, just as it is easier to learn a foreign language in a country where that language is spoken. Not every foreigner living there will learn it, but they have the advantage of their environment to speed and facilitate their learning. All else being equal, even the least diligent student there is better situated over the person studying back home in a classroom, even if they don't take advantage of it.

By going through my own extended season of lack, I was able to write the following in an email to a friend: "Having experienced both now, I can say unequivocally that it is bitter beyond comparison to have all that you want but to grasp for the Lord and not feel his presence than to rebound from heartache to heartache experiencing him at your side."

God met me in powerful ways amid my need. Not always with the outcome I'd first hoped for, but with something better: himself. Over time, he became my most hoped-for outcome of every trial. Isaiah 25:4 says, "For you have been a stronghold to the poor, a stronghold to the needy in his distress, a shelter from the storm and a shade from the heat." A stronghold was needed; a stronghold he was.

Just as we may try to conceal our lack from others, we may also hesitate to be open about our limits. Acknowledging either requires humility and trust. But just as lack can bind us more closely to God and community, so can limits. Limitless living is not living life to the full; it is bleeding life dry. Without acknowledging or honoring our limitations, frustration and burnout will follow.

And of the gift of limits, Peter Scazzero writes in *Emotionally Healthy Discipleship*,

> A limit is a gift few of us want. The question is why?
>
> The answer is twofold. First, almost everything in the messaging coming from the wider culture resists this countercultural truth found so clearly in Scripture. And secondly, it touches on the root of our rebellion against God, just as it did for Adam and Eve in the garden.

And yet, limits offer us so many gifts. They protect us so we don't hurt ourselves, others, or God's work. They keep us grounded and humble, reminding us we are not in charge of running the world. They break our self-will. They are God's means to give us, and our ministries, direction—if we will listen. They are one of the primary ways we grow in wisdom.[10]

God is not pleased, enjoyed, or honored when we blow past our limits and act like gods. Recognizing our limits is not just assenting to the reality of who we are as finite but to who God is as limitless. Fierce independence is not just a rejection of our design but of his grace. Yet when limits are embraced for the gifts they are, they shield us from needless toil and usher us into a world of God honoring, neighbor-uplifting interdependence.

Reflection Questions

1. Read Psalm 90:12 and James 4:13. Which one of these mindsets best aligns with your natural tendencies?

   _____

   _____

   _____

   _____

2. What are your Sabbath practices? How does your understanding of limits play into how you observe the Sabbath—or if you're not in the practice of observing it, how might God be calling you to change your approach?

   _____

   _____

   _____

   _____

3. What do you consider materialistic, and where do you draw that line? What kind of controls do you have in place in your life to ensure you do not fall into that sin?

   _____

   _____

   _____

   _____

4. From a worldly perspective, what are the advantages to being independent?

   _____

   _____

   _____

   _____

5. Are you more likely to be vocal about your needs or keep them to yourself? If you're more likely to keep them to yourself, what makes you hold back?

_____

_____

_____

_____

6. What ministries within your church address people with problems with materialism or those who struggle to share their neediness for whatever reason?

_____

_____

_____

_____

6

DEVOTION
The Gift of Singleness

I say to the LORD, "You are my Lord;
apart from you I have no good thing."
LORD, you alone are my portion and my cup;
you make my lot secure.
The boundary lines have fallen for me in pleasant places;
surely I have a delightful inheritance.

PSALM 16:2, 5-6 (NIV)

I can picture it now. You've been tracking along in the book, nodding your head every now and then, underlining here and there, but now you've turned the page to see a chapter on singleness. If you're married, you may think this no longer applies to you, so you'll pass. Or, if you're still single, you roll your eyes and contemplate briefly whether you, too, want to choose your own adventure and just skip to the next chapter. That's what I would do. The *last* thing you want to hear about is how this thing that is so abjectly unsatisfying to you—the source of your loneliness, anxiety, insecurity, restlessness, and doubt—could possibly be a gift.

But, reader, that is what every single one of these chapters has been about.

What makes this different?

Well, for one thing, your singleness is always with you. It is there when you sit, rise, and lie down. If you ascend to heaven, it is there! If you make your bed in Sheol, it is there! Goodness, if you take the wings of the morning and dwell in the uttermost parts of the sea, even there, singleness shall find you and keep you firmly in its grip. That's how that verse goes, right?

Answer: no! Singleness is not God. God is God. And even if you end up dwelling permanently in the Land of Not Marrieds, even there his hand shall lead you, his right hand—valiant, supportive, shade-giving, glorious in power, of bottomless pleasures—shall hold you firm.

This chapter belongs to the section on gifts of dependence—as it should—because if you're going to survive singleness, it will take nothing short of the power of God. Wait, I'm sensing a theme here.

"But, Alicia, you don't understand the scope of what all my single-ness touches!" Please, I am pushing 40 and can count on two hands the number of dates I've gone on. I understand.

To be honest, this chapter *isn't* that much different from the oth-ers. Other outsiders may feel lonely, anxious, insecure, restless, or wary about some aspect of their identity or circumstances. Or they bemoan the horizonlessness of their difference. Like singles, other outsiders wrestle with their own questions about God's sovereignty and protec-tion and the goodness of his design. Singleness, too, holds as much potential for self-discovery and growth as for pain. So, welcome to the club, fellow unmarried friends. There's grace for you here. (Don't you worry, married friends. There's grace for you here too.)

Singleness may surface doubts you have about your worth and stretch your trust in God. Past a certain age, single people differ from married people in a way that is meaningful both to themselves and to those around them who are no longer in that stage of life. It is a differ-ence based on circumstances that may or may never change.

As friends marry off and seem to retreat into their families or other couples' activities, singleness can seem to prevent us from full participation in our wider community. Many cultures place high value on marriage, and singleness carries stigma and shame. But we are not victims of life's circumstances; we are recipients of special grace, in league not necessarily with those whose lives are brimming with everything they desire, but with Paul: in Christ uncrushable and not driven to despair. Could it be true for us, too, that as truths of God's love for us seep into the hardest-to-reach corners of our identity, we would be able to be witnesses of and to the surpassing power of God? If I have posed the question for other circumstances in life, why not this one: Are all gifts which bring Christ's power to rest on us?

No or Not Yet

I have long enjoyed the rare luxury of belonging to a family where the topic of my singleness doesn't often come up. In fact, I can count on one hand the number of times someone has asked me about it, and as far as I know, there's no "Operation: Get Alicia Married" conversation underway on a secret family text thread.

When I was learning Lao, I was surprised to learn that marriage was so culturally normative that it impacted the acceptable answers to "Are you married?" There were only two: "yes" and "not yet." When I attempted to reply "no" in conversation, I was always corrected.

"Are you married?" packs a punch. More than a simple request for information, it can leave us second-guessing our lives, ourselves, our futures, and our God. It's easy for us to superimpose on that question a cluster of smaller ones: Are you desirable? Is your future secure? Are you lovable? Are you successful? Do you matter? Are you enough? When we answer the marriage question in the negative, whether it's "no" or "not yet," it may feel like a proxy answer for the others as well.

If we can let the other outsider examples teach us anything, it is that there does not need to be any hope of circumstantial change for there to be a heart change. It's true. For the chronically ill and those with disabilities, sickness lingers. For those grieving loss, it may be irreversible. For the persecuted, there's often no regime change in sight. Victims of injustice look generations into the future to the potential for change, and yet we find those who are sick, in mourning, and oppressed relishing their spot at the feet of Jesus.

What's So Great About Being Single?

> I want you to be free from anxieties. The unmarried man is anxious about the things of the Lord, how to please the Lord. But the married man is anxious about worldly things, how to please his wife, and his interests are divided. And the unmarried or betrothed woman is anxious about the things of the Lord, how to be holy in body and spirit. But the married woman is anxious about worldly things, how to please her husband. I say this for your own benefit, not to lay any restraint upon you, but to promote good order and to secure your undivided devotion to the Lord (1 Corinthians 7:32-35).

If I'm honest, my standard answer about what's so great about being single usually starts with freedom, not devotion. I'm challenged to view my singleness first from that lens too. Abounding in singleness—the beautiful and rich gift offered in Christ—goes beyond just learning to enjoy your own company or relishing in your independence. One thing I've found lamentable is that, when I look around, it seems like both the unmarried and the married are equally anxious about worldly things.

I recently embarked on a work project involving a spreadsheet. That spreadsheet became my life, and I couldn't have been happier about it. There's just something I can't resist about a seemingly endless sea of rows and columns. My roommates joked about my "spreadsheet energy," now the stand-in phrase we use to describe complete dedication—undivided devotion, if you will—to a task. When I would call home to catch up with my family, I sent them glamour shots (read:

screenshots) of my spreadsheet. Even though I can't stay up late for anything else, I would get to work on the spreadsheet, and the next thing I knew, it would be two in the morning. This spreadsheet awakened within me a long-dormant *joie de vivre*. I wanted to talk to people at parties about it. I even dreamed about it. In my downtime, I would lovingly look back at the screenshots I'd taken of it. Whenever I wasn't working on it, I couldn't wait to start working on it again. I couldn't claim I didn't have the time or bandwidth to devote myself to anyone or anything else, or that devotion just looked different in my life. Given the right object, my attention and energy were easily captured.

Secure Lots, Pleasant Places

I intentionally didn't choose 1 Corinthians 7's passage on singleness as the key verse for this chapter. Instead, I choose Psalm 16, my favorite psalm. While not directly related to marriage or singleness, it has been my constant companion on the road from single-insecure to single-neutral and finally to single-satisfied, letting singleness better me and draw me to Jesus.

> Keep me safe, my God,
>   for in you I take refuge.
> I say to the Lord, "You are my Lord;
>   apart from you I have no good thing."
> I say of the holy people who are in the land,
>   "They are the noble ones in whom is all my delight."
> Those who run after other gods will suffer more and more.
>   I will not pour out libations of blood to such gods
>   or take up their names on my lips.
> Lord, you alone are my portion and my cup;
>   you make my lot secure.
> The boundary lines have fallen for me in pleasant places;
>   surely I have a delightful inheritance.
> I will praise the Lord, who counsels me;
>   even at night my heart instructs me.
> I keep my eyes always on the Lord.

With him at my right hand, I will not be shaken.
Therefore my heart is glad and my tongue rejoices;
    my body also will rest secure,
because you will not abandon me to the realm of the dead,
    nor will you let your faithful one see decay.
You make known to me the path of life;
    you will fill me with joy in your presence,
    with eternal pleasures at your right hand (Psalm 16).

At its core, Psalm 16 deals with finding satisfaction. But the satisfaction of this psalm is one found less in life expressly than in God himself. Perhaps this is the way to get at satisfaction in life—obliquely, focusing not on life but on God instead. This psalm has taught me about the bigness of God, the closeness of God, the power of God, and the person- and circumstance-specific care of God. It has spoken to my loneliness, insecurity, and wariness about a future for one.

The psalm opens with a declaration of trust. God is a refuge, a safe place, a shield, and defense for the psalmist. It is part plea ("keep me safe") and part confession ("for in you I take refuge"). This psalm overflows with adoration and confidence in God. Not even Sheol itself can prevail. Everything in the world tries to convince us otherwise—either that everything else is better than God, or that God isn't really good; that God is a tool and not a treasure; that God is not trustworthy; and therefore it is natural and acceptable to be shaken by everything undesirable that comes my way.

But my lines have fallen in pleasant places. He makes my lot secure. Apart from the Lord, I have no good thing. Self-sufficiency, independence, and circumventing God's will—chasing after other gods—will add sorrow to sorrow, frustration to frustration. Does sorrow not dwell in the shadow of God's displeasure while satisfaction in the brightness of God's delight? Sheltered in him, I will be neither shaken nor left alone. His presence will fill me with joy. What promises this psalm holds!

Psalm 16 enables me to bring that "spreadsheet energy" to 1 Corinthians 7, seeking to please the Lord.

Anxious About the Things of the Lord

When I was in graduate school, I once visited my art history professor's office to discuss a paper I'd written. It was toward the end of our time together, and he confided that he was envious of students. I asked why, and he said it was because, after graduate school, he'd never again in his life had as much time to just think. *Time to just think?* I thought. *You mean being overwhelmed with readings, translations of pages and pages of Chinese, group projects on end, and other assignments?* And yet after that conversation, I began to consider for the first time that graduate school could be a "time to just think." I was glad he shared that with me before I finished so I could value that time and its purpose accordingly.

I hadn't often thought about my singleness as "time to just be anxious about the things of the Lord," but I'm glad Paul told me that before it ends (if it ever does), so I can value this time and its purpose accordingly.

I recently reached a milestone at work for which my company gives gifts. I've heard my gift is a little Tiffany & Co. container; I've seen a picture of it, and I'm still not clear if it's an ashtray or something for jewelry. Because we are operating with a hybrid work environment, I don't go into the office every day, but I received an email saying that on any weekday except Tuesday I could go pick up my gift. Guess what day I'm in the office? Tuesdays. So far, the gift I was given has gone unclaimed.

Like the high-valued Tiffany ashtray, I can come claim the gift if I want. It's a gift I might not have chosen on my own and is almost certainly more than I can afford. Yet it's sitting in some box in a dark corner of HR. The reality is, it doesn't matter if it's an ashtray or a jewelry box; I can find some way to use it. Sam Allberry writes, "If we balk at the idea of singleness being a gift, it is not because God has not understood us but because we have not understood him."[1]

We make light of our love for the Lord, but it wasn't cheap. Back in the day—think Deuteronomy—our hearts were unable to love God. "But to this day the LORD has not given you a heart to understand or eyes to see or ears to hear" (Deuteronomy 29:4). The theme of loving the Lord appears first in Deuteronomy 6:5 with the command to love: "Love the LORD your God with all your heart and with all your soul and with all your might." Then comes the promise of new hearts with the "love God" function: "I will give them a heart to know that I am the LORD, and they shall be my people and I will be their God, for they shall return to me with their whole heart" (Jeremiah 24:7). Who paid for these new upgraded hearts? Christ did.

This is a covenant blessing that married people have limited capacity to enjoy. Once married, they set about in their new and sacred mission of loving their spouses and kids, if and when the Lord enables their families to grow. They are now people of divided devotion. Not my words, Paul's. A single-minded pursuit of God and commitment to his service is not a consolation prize. We, the unmarried, continue in *our* sacred mission: undistracted adoration. *How can I be more devoted to you today than yesterday? How can I depend on you today to have my needs met and discover new facets of your perfection? How can I experience more of this precious gift you've given me today?* This is the unclaimed gift sitting in some box in a dark corner of HR for most who aren't married. Instead, it's: *How soon can I be free from the burden of undivided devotion? When can I move on from giving my whole heart to you and your affairs?*

Unmarried People in the Church

Singles and other unmarried people are often overlooked in the church. Apart from illustrations and programming that cater to families, singles are the "pick up the slack" group. They are the ones who get stuff done when married members' lives get overfilled with family obligations. When singleness is addressed, it is presented more often than not as the inferior option and even in some circles—for women especially—a dereliction of our call, rather than a lateral move from one sacred mission to the next.

If you're single and living far from family, singleness can be especially hard. When holidays roll around and families busy themselves with traditions, you're left out. This isn't how it's meant to be.

A Family for the Lonely

Here we see once more the double-pronged gift of dependence on God and interdependence on Christian community at work in the gifts. Psalm 68:6 says, "God sets the lonely in families" (NIV).

Married friends, when I said I had grace for you, too, here it is: Your families aren't just yours. As surely as they are the Lord's, they belong to the whole body. Your family is a gift you can give the lonely, in service both to God and to his church—as Peter would say, "as faithful stewards of God's grace in its various forms" (1 Peter 4:10 NIV). To someone who is lonely, your family could very well be one of God's intended forms of grace.

Many years ago, I was walking in a Walmart parking lot with my older sister. A woman approached us, and my sister stopped and greeted her with a big hug. I stood off to the side to watch the exchange. Once the other woman continued into the store, I asked my sister, "How do you know that woman?"

"I don't," she replied. I was confused—the scene I'd just witnessed was, without a doubt, the surprise reunion of old friends, wasn't it? "We belong to the same sorority," she said, "but I've never met her before." At the time, I didn't have a particularly strong relationship with this sister, and here she was, excitedly greeting this "sister" stranger.

Family is not unique to Christians. It has existed across all cultures and times. What *is* uniquely Christian is the family of God. As real as our rebirth and adoption as God's children is our being placed into a larger family, one where there are no only children. John 1:12-13 says, "But to all who did receive him, who believed in his name, he gave the right to become children of God, who were born, not of blood nor of the will of the flesh nor of the will of man, but of God."

Imagine a community where, when others considered what was best for them, that included what was best for you too; where resources were shared not out of compulsion but by an awareness of mutually dependent welfare; where you felt a sense of security knowing your brother or sister truly was your keeper and would strive to keep you as ardently as they kept themselves. Imagine asking yourself if the family you've been entrusted with could be God's answer to one of the lonely among you.

Community

Here's the good news: We are created to be in community with one another. In the early pages of Genesis, God says it is not good for a man to be alone (Genesis 2:18). Even before the fall, we were not meant to go through life alone. The reality is that some of us will never marry. Yet the promise of abundant life is as good for those as it is for those who will.

One of the rare times a family member asked about my singleness was at a family birthday gathering. My uncle said he was worried that when I got old, my friends, my church friends, and what I've done for the church won't be there for me the way a companion would, and that in hindsight, they may matter less than I think they do now. In that moment, I wondered: How had he experienced friendships that made him think this could be true? How had he experienced Christian community? How had he experienced God? Did he know the joy of intimacy with him or serving him?

I sometimes wonder if most people take seriously God's claims about himself. I've certainly had moments like that. I think about Jesus's visit back to his hometown, where he said he could not do miracles there because of their lack of faith (Matthew 13:58). Had I limited my experience of grace by limiting my belief in what I thought it capable of? Had I likewise limited my experience of what he could provide through himself and through the members of his body those times I didn't expect much?

Part of the perks of being in Christ is that we get to experience family even if we lack family. We get to experience pursuit without being pursued. We can be confident of our own worth when the world does not affirm it. How many of us believe things about ourselves primarily because they are externally corroborated—because that's what the culture says about us? But let the tide of public opinion change, let cultural preferences shift; then you will find out if "the taste of the times" was not also just a grain of sand under your house you'd confused for a rock.

Diseased cultures don't get the last word on who you are—even if that unhealth is within the church. I've learned that it is real work to see yourself and your situation through God's eyes rather than the world's. Cultures that elevate marriage over singleness have distorted the truth, but you don't have to give oxygen to their distortions.

I have been spared a lot of the woes many single people go through. I have, for the most part, always had housemates. I have attended churches whose congregants were on the younger side and where we didn't cater as much to families since there weren't many. My own family has put zero pressure on me to get married. I rent, so property management takes care of fixing things around the house. So, I write this chapter as an outlier among outliers, but I see the rest of you out there struggling (or feeling burdened) with home projects, coming home to empty houses—or perhaps to pets—and longing for children and companionship instead.

Nowhere are we promised a second-class experience in life because we are unpartnered. It is not God's "plan B" for us. The promise given to us is the same as that given to everyone else, even as the ache for marriage remains. Questions of "How long?" "When is it my turn?" "Who will help me?" and "Who is looking out for me?" are all legitimate.

One of my episodes of wanting to be married more badly than usual was instigated by learning my grandfather had cancer. I wondered who would be there for me if I reach his age and become ill. It saddened me and after considering that question for a while, I couldn't come up with a single proper noun. Yet God assured me, "Even to your old age and gray hairs I am he, I am he who will sustain you. I have made you and I will carry you; I will sustain you and I will rescue you. With whom will you compare me or count me equal? To whom will you liken me that we may be compared?" (Isaiah 64:4-5 NIV). I had my answer—the most proper of nouns would accompany me.

Our Starting Point

Let's start from the premise that God and his promises are true and can be trusted. Let's be honest about the fact that true promises do not erase the ache. Dan Allender and Tremper Longman write, "Knowing God does not completely take away the emptiness, either. Turning to him can melt away much of our fear, loneliness and pain. But no relationship with God in this present world will ever be as rich, fulfilling or freeing as it will be in heaven. So we are left with a sense of incompleteness, what C.S. Lewis called our 'inconsolable desire.'"[2] Let us also keep vigil for God's right hand—valiant, supportive, shade-giving, glorious in power, and of bottomless pleasures—to hold us and our desires firm as we devote ourselves wholeheartedly to him. What a gift.

As I said, reaching "the inside" is not my endgame. Merely surviving singleness is not it either—rather, my goal is to abound in it. God longs to show us his all-surpassing power right where we are. What if an abounding unmarried person is one who turns to the Lord to provide all they might otherwise attempt to smuggle from a relationship—stability, excitement, significance, identity, healing, worth, and companionship? What if the unmarried sought refuge in the goodness of his will and the sufficiency of his grace against the backdrop of unmet desire or loss?

A Life Not Known Possible

When I worked in Laos, I was a part of a community photography project that worked with artisans who documented the diverse contributions of women to their communities. Through the course of that project, we got to know the women involved very well. One day, we got word that the youngest of the participants, barely a teenager, was going to be married. Her family could no longer afford her school and living expenses. We met as staff to brainstorm how we might be able to intervene to keep this from happening and ultimately ended up offering her an internship at the museum. She helped out here and there, but really, it was a space where she could come and do her schoolwork with minimal interruptions.

Shortly before my contract ended there, the community photography project lead took me aside and told me that the intern had told her she originally hadn't minded the idea of getting married so early and possibly discontinuing school, but then she saw in me a life she hadn't known possible and decided she wanted to complete her studies.

This story often comes to mind when I think about what it means to be a witness for Christ in the world. God is glorified when we live the kinds of lives others had not known possible before. And so it has been my aim, as an unmarried person, to live as an unmarried person in a way others see and say: "I saw in her life a kind of life I hadn't known possible." The kind of life where God alone gets the credit and his power is recognized as further-reaching than previously thought possible.

Reflection Questions

1. In what ways is marriage seen as superior in the church? In society?

   _____

   _____

   _____

   _____

2. If you are unmarried, do you more often see that as a gift to use for the building up of the church or as one to indulge for yourself?

   _____

   _____

   _____

   _____

3. If you are married, what might it look like for you to provide family for those outside of your household?

   _____

   _____

   _____

   _____

4. What aspects of your identity have been malformed by believing the lies culture tells us about marriage?

   _____

   _____

   _____

   _____

5. What do you find most admirable or praiseworthy about Jesus?
   How can you build meditating upon those things into the regular
   rhythm of your life?

   _____

   _____

   _____

   _____

6. Pray through Psalm 16 and ask God to show himself to you in the
   ways he showed himself to the psalmist.

   _____

   _____

   _____

   _____

7

TRUST

When You Can't Believe What You See

Blessed is the man who trusts in the LORD,
whose trust is the LORD. He is like a tree planted by water,
that sends out its roots by the stream,
and does not fear when heat comes,
for its leaves remain green,
and is not anxious in the year of drought,
for it does not cease to bear fruit.

JEREMIAH 17:7-8

Swing dancing, for a season, was my life. Twelve-hour layover in Bangkok? Dance the night away. Conference in Hong Kong for work? Fly in a day early for the lindy hop spot.

I began swing dancing in graduate school and easily spent several evenings a week spinning and swinging away the stress of school. After several months of dancing, I signed up for an advanced class on following techniques that required followers to—among other things—dance with their eyes closed as an exercise in trust.

Over several weeks, we learned to mirror our partners, to wait on their maneuvering us rather than rushing ahead with our own ideas or assumptions. Week after week, our instructor assured us our comfort with uncertainty would grow. We would mature from self-willed dancers into trusting and responsive partners able to be spun and dipped on short notice. In the hands of a skilled lead, the most trusting followers would shine brightest on the dance floor regardless of their skill level. Strong-willed, self-certain followers? Beyond saving. This class required I commit to traveling whatever trajectory my partner set for me, trusting that even my missteps could be repurposed to advance the dance. After all, I alone was in the dark; his eyes were open.

I learned more about following God over those weeks than expected. In my attitude toward God, I was too often that strong-willed, self-certain follower, attempting to do things my own way. Impatient, I believed myself to be helping God with my resourcefulness, when in reality, my impatience was hindering the dance more than poor technique. I realized I could benefit from the words Isaiah spoke to Israel: "Let him who walks in darkness and has no light trust in the name of the LORD and rely on his God" (Isaiah 50:10). Waiting and trust *were* the technique. But when the lights of life dimmed, I grasped for everything but God—that is, until I had nothing else to grasp.

The Gift of Trust

Trust is the third of our gifts of dependence. In speaking of the righteous, the psalmist says, "He is not afraid of bad news; his heart is firm, trusting in the LORD" (Psalm 112:7). Instead of retreating into ourselves or spiraling into anxiety, trust makes us confident and firm-hearted.

Yet trust is a little like patience—both sound good in theory, but the true need for them arises out of adverse circumstances we'd rather avoid. I like the idea of patience, but I don't enjoy the waiting or irritation that triggers its necessity. Similarly, trust sounds warm and cozy until life throws a curveball that puts it to the test.

But there is more to trust than its association with the uncertainties and trials that make it necessary. We are also called to trust in seasons of sorrow, in the aftermath of battles seemingly lost. For Louisa Stead, a family beach outing with her husband and daughter turned into tragedy as a little boy began to drown. Her husband rushed in to save the boy. Both died. In the wake of devastating and irreversible loss, she penned these words about trust:

> 'Tis so sweet to trust in Jesus,
>   and to take him at his word;
>   just to rest upon his promise,
>   and to know, "Thus saith the Lord."[1]

While uncertainty is common to all, some experience more of it than others. Outsiders whose surrounding communities peddle falsehoods about their true worth and flout the values of God's kingdom have frequent opportunity to entrust themselves to God. Their outsider status offers abundant opportunities to ask God to overcome obstacles like stigma, shame, isolation, or lack of societal protections. Navigating systems that weren't built with us in mind brings us time and again back to God for direction. The more we turn to God and choose to take him at his word, the stronger our trust muscles grow.

We also bring different aspects of our life and livelihood before God, so that he might shine new understanding on our circumstances, identity, and worth. Who relies more on God to be their voice than the one who stutters or cannot speak? Who recognizes God as their light better than the one who once sat in darkness? Who credits God as their health but the one with the bleak diagnosis? Who runs to God as their defense but the one with no other advocate or shield? Who knows God as their strength but the one who is weak? Whether because of his sovereignty, his goodness, his power, or his presence, outsiders still faithfully holding white-knuckled to Christ even after trial and heartache have sought God with their questions, and—whether they have found answers or not—have found grace.

Trust helps us weather uncertainties and trials. It steadies us when we're tempted to buy into the world's narratives about our worth and our future. When life's circumstances resurface the dormant *whys*, *how longs*, and *what-ifs* of hearts no longer at ease, trust invites us to rest in the truth of unbroken and unbreakable promises.

Vain Competition

Alternative sources of our trust abound. Scripture speaks to several of Israel's: princes, horses, chariots, fortified cities, the temple, weaponry, Egypt. These "alternatives" distanced them from their ultimate aim. "Behold, you are trusting now in Egypt, that broken reed of a staff, which will pierce the hand of any man who leans on it. Such is Pharaoh king of Egypt to all who trust in him" (2 Kings 18:21). Injuries incurred from trusting Egypt would be self-inflicted. Even David, the slayer of beasts, giants, and tens of thousands, didn't dare trust in himself: "For not in my bow do I trust, nor can my sword save me" (Psalm 44:6). Isaiah warned against misplaced trust as well: "Woe to those who go down to Egypt for help and rely on horses, who trust in chariots because they are many and in horsemen because they are very strong, but do not look to the Holy One of Israel or consult the Lord!" (Isaiah 31:1). The many, the strong, the powerful—when has God ever regarded these as essential to achieving his purposes? Instead, our trust is what he wants.

At our most vulnerable, trust in God alone can strengthen us. Isaiah 30:15-16 says,

> For thus said the Lord God, the Holy One of Israel,
> "In returning and rest you shall be saved;
>   in quietness and in trust shall be your strength."
> But you were unwilling, and you said,
> "No! We will flee upon horses";
>   therefore you shall flee away;
> and, "We will ride upon swift steeds";
>   therefore your pursuers shall be swift.

Though they had witnessed true power, Israel instead trusted these worldly means—all in vain. When Egypt enslaved them, God rescued them, throwing horse and steed into the sea. Yet they rejected true strength—trust—for counterfeits.

Modern-Day Chariots

Our list of where we place our trust today is, in essence, unchanged. As they did with Israel, these alternatives distance us from our ultimate aim as well. We believe our credentials and skills, our connections to those in high places, our abundance of material resources, and our man-made systems will protect us. Our futures will be bright because the research and statistics, the right pedigree, reputation, and financial portfolios suggest so. We even find ourselves praying to an imagined version of our holy God who exists for our comfort and blesses us because we've earned it. Don't all these things sound reliable? If we do everything right, can't we build the lives we want for ourselves?

Even when we recognize these misbeliefs for what they are, it's hard to let them go. Among the "chariots" that bring me a misplaced sense of peace are my own sense of righteousness, my ministry laurels, my political party being in power, my talents, my stable income, my reliable employment. Mistakenly, I, too, often believe that these earthly things have the power to shield me from disappointment and adversity.

A Church Without Trust

Christians who rely on their modern-day chariots rather than the Lord are, according to Jeremiah 17:8, rootless. They panic when heat comes; their leaves wither and brown. In the year of drought, they are anxious; they cease to bear fruit. Their roots grow dry and weak; they are the first to topple in a storm. This is the reality for all who place their trust somewhere other than in the forever faithful Lord God, maker of heaven and earth, the sea, and everything in them. Fear, decay, anxiety, and fruitlessness define such a community even as they sing, raise their hands in worship, attend small groups and church retreats, and even intellectually assent to the doctrine of the sovereignty of God. We need those among us who've had to—as "'Tis So Sweet" puts it—"prove him o'er and o'er."

Yet again, outsiders often offer something unique. Because they lack "chariots" like social connections, financial resources, or institutional support, outsiders almost have no choice but to trust God; they've learned from experience that he is truly the *only* thing that will not let them down. As they preach the goodness of God to themselves, their trust grows:

Though the world would abandon me without second thought, the God who draws near is good to me. Though I am the object of cultural derision, the God who exalts me is good to me. Though my earthly networks are thin, the Lord of Hosts is good to me. Though death is imminent, the God who gives life is good to me.

Even when worldly justice does not prevail, the God of righteousness and justice has my interests at heart. Even when I am hated by the world, the God of love holds me near. Even when others try to silence my cries, the God who hears my every thought listens for my voice. Even though he sometimes responds to my prayers with "no" or "not yet," the God who meets my every need said "yes" when he offered his Son.

Trust grows in the soil of trial and lack. Almost by definition, once you see or receive something, trust is no longer required. God places a premium on being believed in all circumstances. His promises are abundant, and yet our doubts are almost as numerous: We question who he says we are; we don't believe we can access what he says he has given us; we reject his ability to do what he says he will do. We just can't see our way in the dark.

At one point, when the Israelites doubted God's ability to feed them and Moses came before God to complain, the Lord responded, "Is the LORD's arm too short? Now you will see whether or not what I say will come true for you" (Numbers 11:23 NIV). Outsiders are, in a sense, constantly measuring the arm of the Lord with each new obstacle they encounter. In a world that will not recognize our full dignity and beauty, that constantly asks us to prove ourselves and our worth, we return to the identity accompanying our adoption as sons and daughters of the Most High; by God's grace, we remember that we are who he says we are. And by God's very nature, he remains who he says he is.

In an uncertain world filled with gridlocks and detours, God can do what he has said he can do—and we can trust he will not be stymied.

At the end of the day, none of us wants to look like the fool, but that is the fate of those who place their trust anywhere other than God. Though their trust in idols may seem momentarily to have paid off, we can find reassurance in these words in Psalm 25:1-3:

> In you, LORD my God,
>   I put my trust.
> I trust in you;
>   do not let me be put to shame,
>   nor let my enemies triumph over me.
> No one who hopes in you
>   will ever be put to shame,
> but shame will come on those
>   who are treacherous without cause (NIV).

God is never inattentive. He is our ever-present help in our time of need. The great I AM. The unthwartable. And he longs for us to live like we believe that. We may be able to fool our friends into thinking we believe what God says about himself and us. We might even be able to fool ourselves. But we can't fool God. He knows how differently people live when they have taken him at his word—and he can tell when we see him only as a backup in case our self-sufficiency fails.

Earlier we met outsiders Nick, Marlene, Bouangern, and others who—whether their needs be material, emotional, or spiritual—all must learn to trust God. As they find themselves in the dark, they learn to wait on God. Over time, their comfort with uncertainty grows because they come to trust the hands that hold them. Psalm 34:4-5 says, "I sought the LORD, and he answered me and delivered me from all my fears. Those who look to him are radiant, and their faces shall never be ashamed." Fearless and shame-free, they take God at his word. Circumstances cannot convince them God is not who he claims to be. Or that they are worth less than he claims they are worth. These are they who shine bright in the waiting, guided skillfully by their faithful lead.

Reflection Questions

1. What is hardest for you to trust God with? What are you most likely to turn to instead of him? What are your "chariots"?

   _____

   _____

   _____

   _____

2. How do you usually think about trust in the life of the believer? How does your ability or lack of ability to trust God play out in your daily life?

   _____

   _____

   _____

   _____

3. What kinds of things do you think are too small to trust God with? What about too big to trust God with?

   _____

   _____

   _____

   _____

4. Think about a time when someone else's faith encouraged you to trust God. What circumstances were they facing? What made this such a memorable experience?

   _____

   _____

   _____

   _____

5. Think about a time your life circumstances required more trust in God than usual. How and in what ways did God meet you in that experience?

    _____

    _____

    _____

    _____

6. What are some aspects of life for outsiders that you think might require greater trust in God?

    _____

    _____

    _____

    _____

GIFTS OF FREEDOM

Power, comfort, and possessions can carry risks. The following chapters look at the gifts of being free of the strings that come with these.

8

UNATTACHED AND UNAFFILIATED

Uncompromised by Power

When you draw near to the battle, the priest shall come forward and speak to the people and shall say to them, "Hear, O Israel, today you are drawing near for battle against your enemies: let not your heart faint. Do not fear or panic or be in dread of them, for the LORD your God is he who goes with you to fight for you against your enemies, to give you the victory."

DEUTERONOMY 20:2-4

Now we move from gifts of dependence to gifts of freedom—from power, comfort, and greed. Power, comfort, and possessions are not unqualified blessings; sometimes they come with strings and expectations. Distance from them has the power to do us good. The powerful, the comfortable, and the insatiable are all at risk of becoming slaves to the very gifts they possess. What's more, they're burdened by the desire—that often feels like a necessity—to maintain what they've amassed for themselves.

Power has many meanings. For the purposes of this chapter, I define it as the capacity or ability to direct or influence the behavior of others or the course of events. I'm not sure which is worse: the lust for power you've yet to obtain, or the fear of losing the power you currently possess. Both require compromise.

The Bible on Power

It doesn't take long to think of someone whose power got the better of them. Stanford business professor Brian Lowery has a great analogy for this phenomenon: "Think of it as fire. It's useful, but it's also dangerous."[1] Ironically, power often also comes with the fear of man and people-pleasing, two things the Bible roundly condemns that point to the same spiritual problem: valuing how you're judged by others over how you're judged by God. Proverbs 29:25 says the fear of man is a snare, and in Galatians 1:10, Paul states that if he were trying to please men he "would not be a servant of Christ."

With few exceptions, the historical books of the Bible are filled with episode after episode of misused and abused power from the members of the Israelite community to their judges and kings. Unregulated, power has an appetite that's easy to pique but difficult to satisfy. God grants earthly rulers proximate power not for their own personal gain, but for the good of their subjects. Israel's rulers were to uphold the demands of God's covenant and to work for the peace of the people.

Even the best of the judges and monarchs fell short when it came to their use of power. In *Servants and Fools: A Biblical Theology of Leadership,* Arthur Boers writes, "Good rulers are exceptions...Reading the Bible, it is easy to conclude that leadership is *hazardous*...The leadership enterprise is over and again corrupt and corrupting...The prevailing scriptural bias is unremitting suspicion of leaders."[2] But when Jesus came in the flesh, he came not only as Messiah and Christ but as king. Through his life, he demonstrated the proper way to wield power.

In the Bible, those most likely to be without "power" were the poor, the widows, women, orphans, foreigners, and people who had disabilities. These people lacked both the social standing to direct or influence the behavior of others and access to those who could do so on their behalf.

In a church, power is concentrated at the top in its leaders. From a societal standpoint, elected officials, law enforcement, and the wealthy may have more power than others who struggle to make ends meet or live in certain neighborhoods. Regardless of where it is found, all power is derivative. Romans 13:1 says, "For there is no authority except from God." Proverbs 21:1 provides a similar sentiment: "The king's heart is a stream of water in the hand of the LORD; he turns it wherever he will."

For God's children, regardless of how much power we have here on earth, we have unrestricted access to power from above. Every time I pray, I marvel at having an audience with the Creator of the universe. It amazes me that, as Hebrews 4:16 says, we can "with confidence draw near to the throne of grace, that we may receive mercy and find grace to help in time of need."

Power and Outsiders

If God's power is available to all Christians, what is so special about how outsiders relate to power? Power can take you far in this world; without it, the road is marked with obstacle upon obstacle. When life goes awry, the powerless are often at the mercy of others. They lack the social capital or connections to get things done. On any given day without a second thought, decisions are made by those in power that may adversely affect the powerless who either just live with the consequences of those decisions or face more than their fair share of setbacks when they advocate for change.

Earlier, we saw that one feature of an outsider is that in some cases their freedoms are limited due to their social status. Money is one powerful way to end up with more connections, so those who are poor may lack power. Those who, for whatever reason, cannot speak for themselves may also lack power. I live in DC, and it feels like power comes down to whichever party is in office.

There is also a type of social cachet that comes with having the right combination of characteristics. Maybe you possess qualities our culture sees as desirable—youth, beauty, charisma—that allow you to influence the behavior of others or the outcome of a situation; meanwhile, someone without these qualities isn't afforded the same level of privilege and access.

But power comes with strings. Keeping it often requires compromise. Once you have it you may never have enough of it. You may begin to think of yourself differently, perceiving yourself as more capable, worthy, or valuable than those without power. You are accountable to people for money you've received, or you have constituents to keep happy. You're self-conscious about being seen as weak, flawed, or vulnerable; you become afraid of losing your power.

Power changes us. And only very rarely for the better. In *Corruptible: Who Gets Power and How It Changes Us*, global politics professor Brian Klaas confirms what we tend to know intuitively about power,

> A laundry list of studies show that gaining power tends to make people behave in worse ways. The powerful interrupt others more, stereotype more, use less moral reasoning when making decisions, and are more judgmental of behaviors in others that they themselves exhibit. The scientific evidence is occasionally blurry on precisely *why* having control over others affects us so negatively, but few studies suggest that power makes people more virtuous.[3]

It may be easy to envy the powerful. Doors that wouldn't open for others seem to open for the privileged, and issues that would take others months to handle seem to automatically resolve for the powerful—but I would rather be saved from conceit, pride, or the constant craving for more power.

On the flip side, not having power does not have strings—in some ways, it even has advantages. When you have no power and no hope of gaining it, your decision making can't be clouded by the fear of losing it or the desire to expand it. Those without power do not experience the pull toward corruption in the name of self-preservation that power frequently carries. The person managing an empire has a lot more to lose than the person living a quiet life minding their own business (1 Thessalonians 4:11-12). Because the powerless often have less access to external sources of support, help, or comfort, they may be quicker to seek God as an advocate. The powerless may also be able to better understand other individuals coming from backgrounds or circumstances where they've lacked power, even if that circumstance is different from their own. For believers, our lack of control or influence allows us to experience the power of God moving the hearts of other powerful people on our behalf, leading us to lean into learning about God as king, Lord, and sovereign.

That God is above the rulers, principalities, and all powers active in the world is a comfort. But too often we treat God's resources like consolation prizes when that couldn't be further from what they truly are.

The Example of Jesus

Jesus showed us how to properly use power and best exemplified what power should do to people inside of the church. Unlike the powerless, his right view of power didn't come from him being unattached or unaffiliated. He was attached and affiliated to two things: his Father and sinners. Yet he did not go out of his way to move up the ranks of the religious Jewish elite. Despite what some of his disciples wanted for him, he was not drawn to earthly power or tempted to establish his reign here on earth. As the all-powerful king, he submitted to others. He never used his power to abuse or manipulate. He didn't try to amass power in ways that went outside of God's will, and he risked becoming unpopular when doing so was best for the gospel.

When Satan met with Jesus in the desert to tempt him, one of the things he tried to tempt him with was with power—though, of course, this was not how Jesus was supposed to acquire what would eventually be his. Satan made Jesus an offer: "'All these I will give you, if you will fall down and worship me.' Then Jesus said to him, 'Be gone, Satan! For it is written, "You shall worship the Lord your God and him only shall you serve"'" (Matthew 4:9-10).

This temptation is on the table for many—we want the world, and we might be willing to do just about anything to get it, but "what good is it for someone to gain the whole world, yet forfeit their soul?" (Mark 8:36 NIV). Jesus's answer to Satan proved he was not interested in power ill gained.

Later, as Jesus was dying on the cross, he was taunted by onlookers: "The people stood by, watching, but the rulers scoffed at him, saying, 'He saved others; let him save himself, if he is the Christ of God, his Chosen One!' The soldiers also mocked him, coming up and offering him sour wine and saying, 'If you are the King of the Jews, save yourself!'" (Luke 23:35-37) .

Jesus very well could have used his power to come off the cross, but he didn't. He was a savior on a mission and would not compromise, take shortcuts, or be self-serving. He proved it was humanly possible to deny the frequent temptations that accompany wealth, status, and power, even as he had a right to them.

A Foil to the Powerful

If Jesus shows us the correct use of power, then the prophets show us how to be faithful without it. To counter judges, monarchs, and other rulers in the Bible, God instituted a special office of outsiders: prophets. Rather than consolidating influence by might, the prophets' power came from God. "Not having much official power, prophets adopted outsider or 'underside' perspectives. They were frequently rejected, not only by the powers-that-be but by the populace as well…They had an important role and were *the* major counterbalance to the monarchy's power," Arthur Boers explains. "In many ways, they were more important than kings. Their prominence shows a remarkable prioritizing of dissent and critique, especially against the rulers and other leaders."[4]

Prophets were major players in God's redemptive story, from

challenging and counseling rulers, warning the populace of their need to repent, advocating for loyalty to God's covenant, and holding kings accountable—these institutionally powerless individuals stuck close to God and spoke the very words of God boldly. Their outsider status meant that their only allegiance was to the Lord. Their outsider perspective gave them greater freedom to speak from a singular interest: promoting fidelity to God's laws. They neither had the interest nor the means to amass for themselves those things which tempted the traditionally powerful. Despite their relatively low status, God used them to keep his people on track, to point out where they'd gone astray. Prophets, their warnings, their perspectives, and their bold dissent were gifts to God's people, even if they remained unappreciated.

As we consider our standing within our communities—whether we are insiders with power or among those without—we can look to Jesus, both prophet and king, as our example. Jesus also spoke truth to power—warning, coaxing others to repent and return, and calling out misuse of power and authority. And, freed from traps that accompany power, so can we.

Reflection Questions

1. How have you seen power abused?

    _____

    _____

    _____

    _____

2. What are some spheres of your life where you have power?
    How do you approach them? What kind of leader would others
    describe you as?

    _____

    _____

    _____

    _____

3. Are you a people-pleaser or susceptible to peer pressure? How
    might the gospel or Scripture help with one or the other of these?

    _____

    _____

    _____

    _____

4. What relationships in your life come with strings?

    _____

    _____

    _____

    _____

5. In your everyday life, within your normal spheres of influence, how are you tempted to misuse power or authority? Or lord your power over others?

_____

_____

_____

_____

6. Do you tend to think of God as your frontline defense or a last resort? Which of your values might need to be reshaped for you to treasure in your heart all he has offered you?

_____

_____

_____

_____

7. How might the knowledge of God's authority calm anxious thoughts? Which verses in Scripture can you revisit when you feel defeated by your lack of control over the outside world?

_____

_____

_____

_____

9

DISCOMFORT
Freedom from Comfort

*For the moment all discipline seems painful rather
than pleasant, but later it yields the peaceful fruit of
righteousness to those who have been trained by it.*

HEBREWS 12:11

While I absolutely treasured my time in Laos, they were two of
the most physically uncomfortable years of my life. I used to
loathe hot weather, but there I was in the tropics, having bid adieu to
my winter wardrobe. I hated bugs too, though I wasn't one to cry or
jump at the sight of them. I have bad lungs and unexpectedly had difficulty breathing throughout most of my time there. I sometimes had
to sit on the side of the road for half an hour to catch my breath just
from walking, and the sound of my own wheezing would often wake
me up at night. In fact, breathing without thinking about it topped
my list of things I was most looking forward to when I returned to the
US. Beyond that, frequent power outages resulted in lots of lost work,
and a poor internet connection made it hard to keep in touch with
my family in the beginning as I learned how best to access the internet.

Although my breathing never much improved, I came to relish hot weather and conquered my hatred of bugs. Frequently saving my work became second nature, and I found ways to connect to the internet (even if they involved standing as close as possible to other, better-wired homes without raising suspicion). Some discomforts I came to live with, while others I no longer considered as such.

Many of my most formative experiences with discomfort happened abroad, but I realized soon enough exotic locales weren't required. When I lived in Boston, I chose to attend a church precisely because it made me a little uncomfortable. They emphasized certain topics other churches I'd attended had never given much treatment. A decade later in DC, I chose a small group specifically where I knew I'd be an outlier, where I might not catch all the cultural references, and where the majority held worldviews different from mine. They were a group of people I'd often painted in broad strokes, but I thought closer fellowship with them would give me a more detailed picture.

Wherever one encounters discomfort, our reactions to it shape us. Discomfort can refine or break us; we can adapt to it or allow it to incapacitate us. It doesn't have to put us to flight, but instead can ready us for action. Each time I've gone head-to-head with discomfort, I've learned it needn't undo me.

At the closing banquet of a work conference I attended in Bali, I stood in a circle talking with others I'd met over the previous days from other parts of the world that also experienced the frequent power outages I'd encountered in Laos. That evening, the power went out. Suddenly, every conference attendee was thrust into darkness. Those from countries with more reliable electricity became panicked about fixing the power. Their mingling ground to a halt. *What will become of the evening? How soon can we fix this?* As for my little circle, we carried on unfazed, enjoying each other's company in the dark.

"Good" and "Bad" Discomfort

Discomfort comes in myriad shapes and sizes. Physical or cultural conditions can make us uneasy. A clash in values or expectations may set us on edge. Inconveniences may lead to awkwardness, irritation, or surprise. Deliberate hostility, abuse, violated boundaries, conviction and remorse over sin, rebuke, and discipline all might cause discomfort. So, too, can misunderstandings, misrepresentation, or inappropriate comments others make, whether intentional or not. Discomfort also arises from expectations others have of us, either too high or too low. Denying yourself for someone else's benefit, returning kindness for insensitivity, or persevering in righteousness when others don't follow the rules aren't exactly pleasant either. Experiencing the consequences of unchecked sin or receiving spiritual discipline are both kinds of discomfort. Yet the nudging of the Holy Spirit or words of redirection from a Christ-minded mentor are not unpleasantries to persevere against—instead, they should inspire change.

Some discomforts can be greeted as opportunities to practice patience, trust, and compassion—demanding we learn to endure, adapt, and grow—while others can alert us to danger ahead and can harm us if we stoically try to stick things out. In *Emotionally Healthy Discipleship*, Pete Scazzero presents a helpful framework that can be easily adapted for discerning the difference between good and bad discomfort. He writes: "How do I know if meeting this need is a 'good hard' that comes with following Jesus, or if it's crossed the line into a 'destructive hard' that damages my soul and perpetuates immaturity in others?"[1] While he's referring to situations being hard, the same categories can be applied to what makes us uncomfortable. We should learn to distinguish the good discomfort that comes with following Jesus from the "destructive discomfort" that damages our souls and *perpetuates immaturity in others.*

So what do we endure, and what do we flee? In Matthew 5:39-47, we read,

> I say to you, Do not resist the one who is evil. But if anyone slaps you on the right cheek, turn to him the other

also. And if anyone would sue you and take your tunic, let him have your cloak as well. And if anyone forces you to go one mile, go with him two miles. Give to the one who begs from you, and do not refuse the one who would borrow from you.

You have heard that it was said, "You shall love your neighbor and hate your enemy." But I say to you, Love your enemies and pray for those who persecute you, so that you may be sons of your Father who is in heaven. For he makes his sun rise on the evil and on the good, and sends rain on the just and on the unjust. For if you love those who love you, what reward do you have? Do not even the tax collectors do the same? And if you greet only your brothers, what more are you doing than others? Do not even the Gentiles do the same?

Applying this passage to how we can best love those who persecute us requires prayer and thoughtfulness. Discomfort does sometimes signal the necessity for change rather than perseverance. But this Matthew passage—while *not* advocating for remaining in abusive relationships or shaming anyone into staying somewhere when their safety and well-being are at risk—is calling us to an uncomfortable kind of love rarely given.

We all have people in our lives who are difficult to love, whose mean-spirited, malicious, or manipulative actions and attitudes have hurt us. Environments rife with open hostility, disregarded boundaries, gaslighting, and other forms of abuse may warrant leaving, or at the very least, doing what you can to protect yourself. We can remain in community and ministry with destructive people without unyieldingly placing ourselves in harm's way. It is good and wise to set boundaries to avoid inviting mistreatment, and you get to choose where you set them. However, in situations that are uncomfortable but where we aren't being actively harmed, we must be mindful of how the world can manipulate ideas about "setting boundaries" or "taking care of yourself" to make us believe that putting our own desires first is an effective and essential way of protecting our emotional well-being. I've seen how boundaries can be used to exempt ourselves from patience and forbearance, or as a cover for our own selfishness. Sometimes, we prematurely exit spaces where we should remain. We add to burdens we have been called to lighten. We cut frustrating yet ultimately harmless people off, even though they are due our "extra mile" of love. We stop forgiving at seven. We rely on the causticity of our words to convict others rather than the fervency of our prayers. We refuse to part with either cloak or tunic. And at the end of the day, we excuse these un-Christlike actions by claiming we were simply doing what's best for us, as is our right. "I was just setting boundaries," we tell ourselves as we run from discomfort.

But what is God's grace to us if not the power to remain, to lighten, to love better, to forgive yet again, to intercede, to offer both tunic and cloak to the unworthy out of service to Christ? In *Bold Love*, Dan Allender and Tremper Longman write, "Love is a violation of the natural order of meeting power with power and an affront to the visceral response of shielding our soul when an attacker swings in our direction."[2] Are we not mere tax collectors cosplaying as saints when we make excuses for not loving others well? In 1 Corinthians 13, isn't the first listed among love's attributes *patience*? There is no way around discomfort if one desires to please God.

Called to Discomfort

Difference acquaints us with survivable discomfort. By this I mean that we are exposed to discomfort so often that our tolerance for it grows. We are trained by it. Not that some things ever stop being uncomfortable, but we learn better ways to live with the discomfort. This is part of why I consider discomfort a gift. A person who has a very low tolerance for discomfort because they've experienced less of it, may disobey God on the grounds that something is uncomfortable. But another person who has survived discomfort in the past might be able to endure obstacles better and continue walking obediently with

God through their trials. Discomfort can make us more obedient—or at least, less inclined to choose comfort over obedience.

For outsiders, choosing to participate in a community of folks unlike them and love those who challenge them is often uncomfortable. In some situations, we may want to appeal to personality or gifting as a reason to get out of doing something that makes us uncomfortable. In my two years as a missionary, I always found sharing the gospel to be awkward. Every. Single. Time. I would practice with a friend to try and get over my nerves to no avail. When I spoke to people back in the States about my ministry, many would say they could never do what I was doing because it would be too awkward for them. I don't necessarily think that just because God called one person (me) to be a missionary despite my finding evangelism awkward that he's calling every other person who finds evangelism awkward to serve him in the same way. But sometimes, he asks things of us that don't come naturally. Regardless of whether it's at home or on foreign soil, the Great Commission was given to us all, and wherever we are, we ought to share our faith. When God called Moses to be his mouthpiece before Pharoah, Moses objected because public speaking wasn't really in his wheelhouse. But God didn't accept that as an excuse. Calling and comfort do not always travel in pairs.

Looking to God

As we navigate what discomfort might look like in our relationships with others, we might also consider how to approach God when the source of our discomfort comes from within. I enjoy a good period movie (and even prefer the Keira Knightley version of *Pride and Prejudice*). But at least for me, when I watch them, I find myself struggling to insert myself into the world of the movie. What would *I* have been doing had I lived then? Certainly not waltzing around in a petticoat at the ball. Being asked to imagine myself living in a different time period always leaves me dissatisfied with my limited options.

Meanwhile, in the present day, I must frequently confront less-than-promising statistics based on factors outside my control. I often wonder how far in the future I'd have to live for Black women to be as widely recognized for their beauty and intelligence as women of other colors and ethnicities. When might we reach a time when we don't have to work twice as hard for half the credit? These questions, too, are forms of discomfort.

I took my questions and self-pity to God, the clay approaching its potter. Isaiah 29:16 says, "You turn things upside down! Shall the potter be regarded as the clay, that the thing made should say of its maker, 'He did not make me'; or the thing formed say of him who formed it, 'He has no understanding'?" I was not made this way because the stock ran low on premium identities. My identity was outside of *my* control, but it most certainly wasn't outside of God's. Yet reconciling a broken world with being a fearfully fashioned display of God's handiwork despite what the world may say often came with tears.

God remains bigger than statistics and the biased perceptions others may have of me. The time and place in which I was born were not incidental, but carefully considered plot points in the story God has authored for my life. Acts 17:26 says, "He made from one man every nation of mankind to live on all the face of the earth, having determined allotted periods and the boundaries of their dwelling place." While I had been preoccupied with the odds of this or that outcome happening, God spoke a better word: "My grace is sufficient for you" (2 Corinthians 12:9). And as balm to a wound, the words of 1 Corinthians 12:24 bring relief to my worries about the ubiquity of anti-Blackness: "But God has so composed the body, giving greater honor to the part that lacked it." My difference gave me a deeper understanding of the beauty and goodness of God's design; my discomfort over how others perceived me allowed me unique insight into his ability to redeem what the world had broken.

Blessed Conviction

Conviction also makes us deeply uncomfortable. When others call us out on our sin, we feel attacked or belittled. No one likes to think there might be something wrong with them, or that their actions or attitudes might put them in the wrong. When called out, we often respond with un-Christlike defensiveness or go on the attack. Maybe we shut down and withdraw, or maybe we rationalize to determine why we either aren't guilty of the charges against us or why those charges aren't so bad after all. But we must start thinking about spiritual rebuke and conviction differently; they make us better, even as they make us squirm. No discipline is pleasant at the time, but those wounds from a friend, the new awareness of sin that comes from being in community with others from a different background, or even attacks from an enemy that sting because they're true—if we allow these things to make us better, then they can be considered gifts too.

I mention conviction in this chapter on discomfort because it's typically an uncomfortable experience that often accompanies figuring out how to live together united in diversity. I don't just say this as a message for the majority, but for the outsider as well. Whoever genuinely makes true unity their aim cannot avoid conviction. But too often, I find people are unwilling to begin on a path that requires the discomfort of first looking deeply and soberly at themselves. Yet conviction is not something to balk at—it is grace.

Surviving Discomfort

We are comfort-seeking creatures, and it's not hard to see why in this age of convenience and options. Why be uncomfortable when you can choose not to? Even as Christians, we often live as if God's greatest commandment was to love comfort with all our heart, soul, mind, and strength. Many people believe they should never have to feel uncomfortable or that discomfort is always a signal they should immediately seek greener pastures. That may sometimes be true, but it isn't a given.

Many passages of Scripture speak to God wanting peace and prosperity for his people. Our cultural tendency toward individualism, however, translates this as God wanting "me," the individual, to feel happy and relaxed all the time, no matter what. If *I* am not comfortable, at peace, and prospering, I'm well within my rights to leave and find my comfort elsewhere. We deserve to be comfortable, don't we? But for me, discomfort has always carried the potential for more than just frustration, awkwardness, and disorientation. I've learned from it as well. Amanda Lang, author of *The Beauty of Discomfort: How What We Avoid Is What We Need*, writes of athletes,

> Viewing [discomfort] as necessary and inevitable not only helps them tolerate it, but also lessens its power over them...The message is clear: believing you can control your feelings of discomfort heightens your ability to cope. And you don't have to be a high-performance athlete for that to be true. If you interpret your discomfort as threatening—or obsess about it instead of focusing on your goal you will suddenly be living in a world of pain. If, however, you view discomfort as necessary, inevitable, and even an encouraging sign that you're on the right track, it just might be your best friend.[3]

All too often, when faced with discomfort, we do not keep our goal in mind. We forget that our greatest privilege is to be formed into the likeness of our long-suffering savior. Some discomfort is necessary and inevitable if one desires to please God.

When we seek God in our discomfort, we learn that nothing is too hard for him or beyond his ability to provide. When we ground our expectation in God alone and endure hard-but-good discomfort long enough to witness the first blooms of righteousness, our tolerance for discomfort grows. We test the depth and breadth of God's grace and our faith by allowing ourselves to call out for his hand rather than seeking immediate escape.

I think of the Israelites in the wilderness, seesawing between doubt and faith in God's merciful provision. With each new set of circumstances they encountered, God would do good to them, but this lesson never stuck. In Psalm 78:18-20, a chronicle of this seesawing, the psalmist writes, "They spoke against God, saying, "Can God spread a table in the wilderness? He struck the rock so that water gushed out and streams overflowed. Can he also give bread or provide meat for his people?" Like Israel, we too often come to God, asking, "Can you also…?" instead of coming expectant, confident that because God has given us water, he will provide for us this time as well. In the same chapter, Israel is described as having forgotten God's works (verse 11), as not believing in God's saving power (verse 22), as being unconvinced by his wonders (verse 32), and as having hearts that were not steadfast (verse 37). When we face "good discomfort" for which the world offers no remedy but retreat, let us remember his wonders and remain steadfast under his tools.

The Call to Discomfort

One night on a trip, my friends and I decided to toast glasses during dinner. A guy who'd lived in China before went to tap his glass against mine—and in China, you honor those of higher status by holding your glass lower than theirs. Both of us kept trying to lower our glasses to honor the other, first lowering our arms, then bending our knees to hunch down, and eventually falling to the ground to see exactly how low we could physically get the glasses. The rest of the room had no idea what we were doing or why we were on the floor, but I always think of this toast when I hear Romans 12:10: "Outdo one another in showing honor." Putting ourselves second—or last—will always be uncomfortable. That is, until you are trained by it.

Consider for a moment if no one in the history of the church ever did anything uncomfortable. Would we have had Paul, who put up with unimaginable discomfort for the sake of the gospel? What if early apostles had kept to their own culture without a care for the Great Commission? Imagine if Martin Luther had chosen not to stir the pot, or if Martin Luther King Jr. had accepted the approach of the white moderate.

Now consider if Jesus had never chosen to experience discomfort. Would Jesus have come and lived among us, disregarding the loss of stature and glory and all the comforts of heaven? Would we have a high priest able to sympathize with us? The fact that discomfort was not beneath Jesus should tell us it's not beneath us either.

I love the *International Children's Bible's* version of Psalm 18:35: "You have stooped to make me great." The Christian Standard Bible translates this verse to: "Your humility exalts me." Sometimes, what we may experience for a moment as discomfort is really our first step toward humility.

Think about your church: Who enjoys the greatest comfort and at whose expense? More often than not, the outsiders are experiencing the lion's share of the discomfort. Think about yourself. Can you think of a time when a little less comfort for you would have resulted in a little more comfort for someone else? How often do you wonder about who the least comfortable person in the room is and what it might take to smooth the way for them, to share their burden? How could you charge their comfort to your account?

God asks us to do many things that will likely take us outside of "comfortable." The sentiment that you don't have to make yourself uncomfortable for anyone simply cannot be supported by Scripture. Becoming all things to all people may cause discomfort. Honoring others above yourself may cause discomfort. Doing good to those who curse you may cause discomfort. Taming the tongue may cause discomfort. Taking the lowest seat may cause discomfort. Bearing with one another may cause discomfort. Taking up your cross may cause discomfort. It's again important to acknowledge that calling and comfort don't always travel in pairs.

We seek to eliminate all discomfort from our lives to our own detriment. In an article for *Counseling Today*, two psychologists explain some of the benefits of discomfort, "When comfort is the only choice, resilience and the ability to overcome adversity are lost."[4] If the church is to be a place where we put others' interests before our own, where we value unity over homogeneity, where we are poised to welcome the vulnerable and advocate their cause, where we can correct others and be corrected in love, where it's a race to the last and lowest places rather than first, and where favoritism has no place, good luck getting there without some discomfort on everyone's part.

Comfort can draw us to much that isn't best for us, and discomfort can cause us to avoid what will do us good. Truly, the kind of community we're called to is an uncomfortable one that asks more of us than we have in ourselves. Paul laments the struggle he sees within himself between the good he knows he should do and wants to do, and the ability of his flesh to act on it: "For I know that nothing good dwells in me, that is, in my flesh. For I have the desire to do what is right, but not the ability to carry it out...Wretched man that I am! Who will deliver me from this body of death? Thanks be to God through Jesus Christ our Lord!" (Romans 7:18, 24-25).

Holy living goes beyond our resources. Even the best-natured of us are called to live beyond ourselves, and not just occasionally, but daily. Christ wouldn't have needed to die had we been able to replicate his kingdom on our own. Why send the Holy Spirit if we can just reach deep down within ourselves and be the right kind of people? But love, joy, peace, patience, kindness, goodness, faithfulness, gentleness, and self-control are ultimately beyond us. If God needed to sacrifice his Son and fill the world with his Spirit for us to know him, love him, follow him, and build up his church, we could never have done so without needing to rely on him for help. We are led to live out a humble, persistent, load-bearing love, not by earthly passions, conceit, or willpower, but by the Spirit alone.

There is a beautiful form of traditional woodworking in Afghanistan called *jali*. I once got to stand inside an Afghan geodesic half-dome made completely of latticed wood with not a single nail in the structure. Arches are notoriously challenging to hold up, but because geodesic domes use triangles in their construction, they're able to divide the stress evenly so the arch can support itself "much like the shell of an egg."[5] How much stronger might the church be if our stress was distributed evenly among the "structure," instead of expecting the weakest members to carry the greatest load and bend to meet peers who won't bend to meet them in return?

I am not off the hook in this quest for unity either. If I weary in the pursuit of true unity to preserve my feelings; if, in buckling under the strain, I capitulate to ease my discomfort rather than look to Jesus who yokes himself with me and offers rest; if I put my hurt feelings before the good of the church; if I am content to abandon the true beauty, well-being, and wholeness of the body because I cannot see with eyes of faith that God brings fruit in his time and in his ways, I am just as guilty of peddling counterfeit peace.

Discomfort does not have to be something we run from like a house ablaze. In my own life, embracing it has brought great gain. Looking to God, I've uncovered the beauty and goodness of his design and his ability to redeem the broken. Trusting that conviction moves me closer to God and godliness and not further from it, I've investigated my own assumptions, confronting where I fall short in how I view others and otherness itself. Through surviving a lot of discomfort and coming out the better for it, I've realized that a life of discipleship cannot be lived entirely within one's comfort zone and that perhaps the richer soil for growth is found at its outskirts.

Reflection Questions

1. What situations make you most uncomfortable? And what is your usual response to that discomfort?

   _____

   _____

   _____

   _____

2. Recall a time when discomfort led you to a discovery about God or yourself.

   _____

   _____

   _____

   _____

3. In what ways can obedience be uncomfortable? Or, which of God's commands feel most uncomfortable, undesirable, unpleasant, or inconvenient for you to obey? How might this discomfort be a sign that you are growing in faith and perseverance?

   _____

   _____

   _____

   _____

4. From seeking freedom from a sinful habit to taking up the call of a new ministry, consider a time when the "discomfort" of the Spirit's conviction led you to make a difficult change in your life. What did you learn about God from this experience? How did it lead you to grow in faith?

   _____

   _____

_____

_____

5. Based on your experience with discomfort that prompted perseverance and discomfort that prompted change, how are you able to discern the difference between the two? What role does prayer play in this consideration?

_____

_____

_____

_____

6. How often do you wonder about who the least comfortable person in the room is and what it might take to share the burden of discomfort?

_____

_____

_____

_____

7. What are small steps you could take to increase your "comfort" with discomfort?

_____

_____

_____

_____

OPENHANDEDNESS

Generosity and Hospitality

We want you to know, brothers, about the grace of God that has been given among the churches of Macedonia, for in a severe test of affliction, their abundance of joy and their extreme poverty have overflowed in a wealth of generosity on their part. For they gave according to their means, as I can testify, and beyond their means, of their own accord.

2 CORINTHIANS 8:1-3

I love gum. In fact, I love it so much that I earned the nickname Doublemint on a summer mission trip because I ate—yes, you read that right, ate—a 15-pack of Doublemint gum during a 30-minute meeting. (And yes, I do have the Amazon of chewing gum trees growing in my stomach.)

In high school, I remember asking classmates for gum all the time. And all the time I would get the same answer: "It's my last piece." I'd think to myself, *What's your point? Didn't you just finish the entire rest of the pack? You had five pieces but can't spare the last one? So stingy!*

We all have our go-to excuses for why we can't give more. Either we find a gift too important to give or the requester not important enough to give to. Yet in the gospel, we see a treasure of matchless worth given to rebels and riffraff. God gave us far more than the last of many things dear to him. God, the Father, did not have one Son *left* amongst a pack of others, but one Son *only*. And yet he was undeterred in giving him to us. Jesus was the unspared only. The one precious beloved Son given for us, not withheld due to his worth but offered precisely because of it. Romans 8:32 says, "He who did not spare his own Son but gave him up for us all, how will he not also with him graciously give us all things?" In the giving of his Son, God demonstrated his complete openhandedness toward us.

The last of our gifts of freedom is that of openhandedness. While chapter five looked at lack as a grace-filled reminder of our neediness and the dangers of materialism, this chapter looks at generosity and finding freedom from greed and selfishness.

Gift-Giving and Godliness

Gift-giving is one of my love languages. One of my favorite things about giving gifts is how the act itself points to God. When I sit down to consider what someone else wants, needs, or would be blessed by, then give it to them without expecting any kind of repayment, I am reminded of God's deliberateness and joy at being able to give gifts to his children. There is something exhilarating about a true gift with no hint of reciprocal obligations. In Acts 20:35, Paul reminds the Ephesians of an important truth: "Remember the words of the Lord Jesus, how he himself said, 'It is more blessed to give than to receive.'" The idea that it is better to give than to receive resonates with me because my own acts of giving provide a window into the giving heart of God.

This feeling would have been completely foreign to the Greco-Roman audience of the New Testament. The Greco-Roman world was notorious for the expectation of reciprocity being baked into their gift-giving eco-system. This extended to the relationship between humans and gods as well. However, Judaism was different. In his exhaustive work on Paul's understanding of gift-giving as it relates to grace, *Paul and the Gift*, John Barclay notes, "It is often and rightly noted that the Torah's legislation regarding the poor, the widow, and the orphan created a Jewish ethic of 'almsgiving' that was distinctive in the ancient world both in its focus on the poor *qua poor* and in the profile that it gave to almsgiving as a virtue."[1] Judaism asked people to give with no expectation of a return.

Being Made Generous

One morning several years ago, I woke up and got dressed to be fired. My office was going through layoffs, and I was the newest and weakest member of my team. I had been hired just six months prior, after 15 long, hard months of unemployment and temp work. When the afternoon came, people began being called to HR, and the office devolved into chaos. Everywhere you looked people were sobbing, packing up desks, or surveying cubicles for survivors. Meanwhile, I sat and awaited my notification. It didn't come. When the day ended, I realized I'd been spared.

I walked home that day in the confidence-boosting navy sheath I'd put on hours earlier in an effort to blunt the force of a blow that would have—had it ever arrived—cast me back into my former joblessness. But instead of this familiar misery, I was overwhelmed by fresh feelings of relief and gratitude.

Under the influence of fresh mercy, I walked past my neighborhood grocery store and encountered a woman sitting outside on the ground, legs sprawled, torso hunched, asking for help. Never have I given as generously to a stranger as I did that day. In *Ministries of Mercy: The Call of the Jericho Road*, Tim Keller writes:

> Mercy is spontaneous, super bonding love which comes from an experience of the grace of God. The deeper the experience of the free grace of God, the more generous you become. This is why Robert Murray M'Cheyne could say: 'There are many hearing me who now know well that they are not Christians because they do not love to give.

To give largely and liberally, not grudging at all, requires a new heart.'"[2]

Perhaps this is the impulse behind "paying it forward." Receivers become givers and then beget new receivers who then become givers. Rinse and repeat. Even what you consider costly transforms when you've just received something that cost someone else. I like to think receivers become givers not so much because they owe someone else, but because they want to recreate for someone else the experience of being caught off guard by naked generosity.

The Bible mentions two exemplars of giving who began with not much to give: the churches in Macedonia who gave out of their extreme poverty mentioned at the start of this chapter, and the widow with just two mites to her name, both of which she gave as an offering. Jesus watches as she places her two mites into the treasure, on the heels of several well-off men who have offered a much larger dollar amount. Comparing the weight of the sacrifices, Jesus says, "Truly, I tell you, this poor widow has put in more than all of them. For they all contributed out of their abundance, but she out of her poverty put in all she had to live on" (Luke 21:3-4).

These people were oriented toward their money—and their Lord—in such a way that they could joyfully give beyond their means. Their circumstances likely meant that they experienced more keenly the sheer openhandedness of God as he provided for them in their extreme need. But we don't have to be poor to be in tune with the fact that at every moment we exist on this divine, glory-declaring mound of creation, we experience God's openhandedness and astonishing mercy. In a way, they're like gravity: discreetly exerting their force on us all in the background, impacting our every movement without drawing attention to themselves. Hebrews 1:3 says, "He upholds the universe by the word of his power." Oftentimes, the outsiders who have, in their desperation, entrusted themselves fully to God are more keenly aware of how they're being upheld.

The Gift of Openhandedness

It's easy to see how openhandedness would be a gift. After all, it is better to give than to receive. Being generous benefits the giver because godliness itself is great gain. Further, the Bible reserves no accolades for those who are not. First John 3:17 says, "But if anyone has the world's goods and sees his brother in need, yet closes his heart against him, how does God's love abide in him?" If being closed-hearted toward our neighbor is a serious enough offense to question whether God's love has indeed taken root in us, then being openhanded appears to be fruit of the effectual work of God on our heart and life. Craig Blomberg writes,

> Contentment in having enough, even without having a lot, is desperately needed in our world. But this, too, turns out to be a timeless challenge, as Proverbs 14:30 reveals: "A heart at peace gives life to the body, but envy rots the bones." The very next verse proves particularly intriguing: "Whoever oppresses the poor shows contempt for their Maker, but whoever is kind to the needy honors God." Given the antithetical parallelism between the rest of the two statements, it appears that the opposite of generosity is oppression! In other words, withholding one's surplus from needier people is a form of subjugation just as surely as more active mistreatment of them.[3]

The opposite of generosity is oppression! We live in a culture where *oppression* is a loaded term, yet here we see the Bible use it in a scenario most of us wouldn't. Having enough yet choosing to withhold calls into question our knowledge of God. Deciding not to give is not merely negligent, but cruel.

The Old Testament takes up this theme as well with the year of jubilee. Deuteronomy 15:9-11 says,

> Take care lest there be an unworthy thought in your heart and you say, "The seventh year, the year of release is near,"

and your eye look grudgingly on your poor brother, and you give him nothing, and he cry to the LORD against you, and you be guilty of sin. You shall give to him freely, and your heart shall not be grudging when you give to him, because for this the LORD your God will bless you in all your work and in all that you undertake. For there will never cease to be poor in the land. Therefore I command you, "You shall open wide your hand to your brother, to the needy and to the poor, in your land."

In the examples of the Macedonians and the widows, we do not see the kind of calculating, begrudging restraint described above but its opposite. The difference is all the starker given the circumstances of each.

Dangers of Greed

Statistically, greed is more likely to impact wealthier people. Please note, I am not trying to demonize wealthy people, nor am I equivocating wealth with greed. However, recent studies have examined the attitudes of the rich toward money, and in particular, psychology professor Paul Piff has researched the psychology of wealth extensively. His research has shown that the wealthy "are more likely to moralize greed and self-interest as favorable, less likely to be prosocial, and more likely to cheat and break laws if it behooves them."[4] But Piff has also said he can sympathize. "We all, in our day-to-day, minute-by-minute lives, struggle with these competing motivations of when or if to put our own interests above the interests of other people," he says. "That's understandable—in fact, it's a logical outgrowth of the so-called 'American dream.'"[5]

Even within his findings on wealth, there was positive news. While wealth certainly impacts people psychologically, "small nudges in certain directions can restore levels of egalitarianism and empathy," Piff says. "Simply reminding wealthy individuals of the benefits of cooperation or community can prompt them to act just as egalitarian as poor people." An underlying key point from this is that poor people tend to be naturally more egalitarian in considering others' interests. "Researchers explain that the rich tend to rationalise their advantage, and believe that they deserved it. They pursue their self-interest and moralise greed easily. The misuse of power and privilege and growing unethicality in societies is increasingly seen as arising from such attitudes."[6]

Proverbs 28:25 says, "A greedy man stirs up strife, but the one who trusts in the LORD will be enriched." Given the parallelism in these verses, it's safe to say that the greedy man does not trust the Lord. We remember from chapter seven what happens to people who place their trust in the wrong people and things. In 1 Corinthians 6, Paul lists categories of people who will not inherit God's kingdom. The greedy are among them. Herbert Schlossberg writes in *Idols for Destruction*,

> The mammon described here as the rival of God, therefore, is the idolatrous elevation of money and the material possessions it will buy as the goal of life. The common expression that describes such a value system as "the pursuit of the almighty dollar" is soundly based in the recognition of the exaltation of possessions to the level of ultimacy is the end of a religious quest, one that seeks and ascribes ultimate meaning. Like all idolatries, it finds ultimate meaning in an aspect of the creation rather than in the creator. And like all idolatries it finds outlet in destructive pathologies that wreck human lives.[7]

Openhandedness as a Reflection of Jesus

The generosity of Jesus was on a scale never seen before and never to be seen again. He has been generous in every possible way: with his body, with his time, with his resources, with his wisdom, with his power, with his very life. He chose to become sin for us, to be obedient unto death, to part with the comforts of heaven, to take up the cross, to heal, to serve people who should have been serving him.

The same grace and mercy that lead people to open their wallets can lead us to open our homes. Hospitality is also an important outward expression of openhandedness—open-homedness. Both are driven by the desire to be generous and to relieve others' burdens. Hospitality in Middle Eastern culture was more than a meal. It was protection and sanctuary as well. Old Testament scholar Gerald Wilson provides depth to the concept as practiced in the Ancient Near East, writing, "To accept another as a guest at one's table was to set aside enmity and to assume responsibility for the safety of the guest while in your dwelling."[8] Hospitality was a call to peace, safety, and grace. It required an openness of heart and home as well as resources.

But hospitality was more than about just entertaining others and looking after their safety. There was a moral component baked into it where it was once viewed as an act of obedience to a God who also opened his doors to us. In *Making Room: Recovering Hospitality as a Christian Tradition*, Christian ethicist Christine Pohl writes,

> For the most part, the term "hospitality" has lost its moral dimension and, in the process, most Christians have lost touch with the amazingly rich and complex tradition of hospitality.
>
> Today when we think of hospitality, we don't think first of welcoming strangers. We picture having family and friends over for a pleasant meal…Hospitality is a nice extra if we have the time or the resources, but we rarely view it as a spiritual obligation or as a dynamic expression of vibrant Christianity.[9]

Being hospitable and generous are fruits from the same tree. A concern for the needy, willingness to be open with your resources, and love for God drive them each.

Reflection Questions

1. What does your current practice of generosity look like? How did it come about?

   _____

   _____

   _____

   _____

2. Can you think of a time when being the recipient of mercy or grace made you more generous?

   _____

   _____

   _____

   _____

3. How do you connect your daily story to the story of God's mercy and grace? What are some practices that could help you do this better?

   _____

   _____

   _____

   _____

4. What could help you be more openhanded?

   _____

   _____

   _____

   _____

5. How does the openhandedness of God encourage you to be openhanded with others?

_____

_____

_____

_____

6. In your family and social circles, what is the culture around gift-giving? Are there usually strings attached?

_____

_____

_____

_____

7. Given that our giving is supposed to be done in secret without drawing attention to ourselves, how might you be able to encourage others by your openhandedness in a way that still communicates your trust in God as you give?

_____

_____

_____

_____

GIFTS OF SUFFERING

In his inscrutable wisdom, God sometimes uses suffering to shape us in his likeness. The next section looks at the gifts of endurance, lament, and grief over injustice.

11

ENDURANCE
The Persecuted Church

*Blessed are those who are persecuted for righteousness' sake,
for theirs is the kingdom of heaven.*

MATTHEW 5:10

When I first showed the table of contents to this book to a friend, she looked at the categories of gifts and said, "These all look like things I'd want, except for the suffering." Understandably, it can be a hard sell.

First, though, it bears saying that our suffering brings God no delight. Lamentations 3:33 (CSB) says, "For he does not enjoy bringing affliction or suffering on mankind." Psalm 116:15 says, "Precious in the sight of the LORD is the death of his saints." And yet, Jesus calls blessed those who are persecuted for his sake.

As I mentioned in chapter one, before our comfort or a change in circumstances, the Christian's goal is to be made like Christ. First Peter 2:20-21 says,

For what credit is it if, when you sin and are beaten for it, you endure? But if when you do good and suffer for it you endure, this is a gracious thing in the sight of God. For to this you have been called, because Christ also suffered for you, leaving you an example, so that you might follow in his steps.

This is the example we are called to follow. We are to be self-sacrificing, right-forfeiting, neighbor-edifying, enemy-blessing carriers of Christ's scent throughout our broken world.

Religious minorities may never, in their whole lives, find reprieve from regimes that would just as soon wipe them clean from the face of the earth. Yet religious freedom is not their endgame because they know it's possible for the gospel and their faith to flourish under persecution. And, in many cases, they look at the church in the US and feel no envy for the corrosive effects of unbridled freedom and cost-cutting privilege on the gospel and faith.

Persecution

Earlier this year, I attended a conference where a non-American woman shared her testimony of being arrested multiple times for her faith. During the Q&A session, someone asked her how she prays for the American church, and she said, "I pray for suffering. It is a grace." Her words reminded me of the answer my college pastor gave me when I asked him what he thought the church most needed for its growth and purification. "Persecution," he responded.

Members of the persecuted church are religious minorities, mostly of the Majority World, who differ from those around them in ways that are meaningful to their surrounding culture. While their difference can be seen as one of choice, their commitment runs deep. For as long as they endure, their outsider status remains. Their worship is unprotected, their freedoms violated, and their safety jeopardized as a result.

Many fear this is where America is headed. The years to come indeed hold challenges for us. Alistair Begg explains what Christians should anticipate and prepare for:

Christians are increasingly going to be seen as different,
and not in a good way. We are increasingly going to have to
choose between obedience and comfort. The next decades
will not bring apathy to the gospel, but antagonism. And
that's OK. After all, that has been the reality for most of
God's people through most of history.[1]

Christians in America and other countries where Christianity
enjoys prominence and influence are ill-equipped for persecution
if and when it comes. What could prepare us? What would induce
someone with a "me first" attitude, someone who can hardly bear
being mocked before choosing malice, bitterness, and pettiness over
Christ, to suddenly hold to Christ in the face of death? How could
someone who thinks so little of the power of the gospel, that it is not
discernable in their love for neighbor, be compelled by that gospel to
die? If they so loved themselves that they couldn't be insulted or misrepresented without declaring through their repayment of evil for evil
that the cross means less to them than they mean to themselves, how
could they choose the cross when the stakes are higher? Will the one
unwilling to cede ground in an argument with their enemy surren-
der their body to them? If pride and impatience are already too steep
a cost for them to take up their cross, how could they afford to part
with their life?

And yet, this is what Christians in parts of the world where it's most
dangerous to be Christian are prepared for every day. In *The Martyr's
Oath: Living for the Jesus They're Willing to Die For*, Johnnie Moore
writes,

> I read something about Americans that I think is true: the
> first rule in our culture is self-preservation. We do every-
> thing in our power to extend our lives, to protect our lives,
> to improve our lives, and to guard our lives, but this is not
> an idea we've inherited from Christianity. The prevailing
> characteristic I have found among persecuted believers is
> not self-preservation but self-sacrifice.[2]

God help us.

As America becomes more secular and the number of Christians declines, we begin to lose some of our privileges within society. But as our faith is less institutionally supported and we are increasingly viewed negatively by our peers, we must see these trials as opportunities to hold to Christ, to bear these costs well, to take up the cross, to reject retaliation, and to practice humility and patience. We need to cultivate the kind of holy imagination that believes the gospel can advance even amid antagonism, and we must reject the mistaken belief that such a hostile world demands we give ourselves over to its principalities to fight our battles for Christ with its weapons.

Between the poles of claiming every slight and loss of privilege as persecution and thinking the church inflicts more persecution than it receives, Karen Ellis, the director of the Edmiston Center that focuses on the study of Christianity on the margins of society, has identified a third way of thinking about persecution among those she speaks to about it. "Hostility realists," she explains, "understand that God has the sovereign ability to accomplish his will in places with more, and with less, religious freedom: he uses each unique set of circumstances in different ways for Kingdom advantage."[3] This is the kind of imagination we need.

Most of us have a very weak theology of persecution. When we encounter passages of Scripture related to it, we don't know exactly what to do with them. We have to recontextualize these verses for us now since the applications for the audience then don't make immediate sense in our low-stakes setting. Or we err by interpreting everything through a persecution lens.

Open Doors, a ministry dedicated to serving persecuted Christians, defines persecution as "any hostility experienced as a result of identification with Jesus Christ."[4] Even though this definition is broad, I believe American Christians label a lot of things as persecution that are not. While we do face changing religious landscapes and demographics, drawing false equivalencies between what different groups suffer helps no one. It makes light of the severe trials our Christian brothers and sisters in places like Afghanistan, North Korea, Yemen, Somalia, and Libya—where they are true outsiders—experience.

In addition to struggling to recognize that we face different levels of discrimination, we also respond to whatever forms of discrimination and loss of privilege we do suffer with a no-holds-barred approach, as though our Savior did not tell Peter to put away his sword (John 18:11). As the religious landscape of America changes, our witness will suffer needlessly if we prioritize defending our own likeability and intelligence to a public that no longer understands our beliefs. Meanwhile, our vengeful, sinful desire to see our opponents suffer will only dilute our ability to embody the power of Christ's grace. We'll be tempted to choose lovelessness as though it were the inevitable response to persecution, and then blame this moral decay on the restrictions to our "liberty" rather than recognize it as our own failing to obey the command to love our neighbor as ourselves. But without love for our enemies, we lie about the very faith we defend. It cannot be faith in the God of the Bible because at least, according to 1 John 4:8 and 20, "Anyone who does not love does not know God, because God is love…If anyone says, 'I love God,' and hates his brother, he is a liar; for he who does not love his brother whom he has seen cannot love God whom he has not seen."

Many Americans have not accurately counted the true cost of following Christ. Centuries of Christianity enjoying institutional support and the shaping of systems to work in our favor have led American Christianity to become the Walmart of Christendom, even while it sees itself as a high-end department store. Our faith comes at a low price. Most Americans are never asked to choose between their Christian faith and their house, family, or land (Matthew 19:29), nor does faith alone often come with the price tag of safety, employment options, or access to public services. In America, the idea of laying down our lives for our faith exists only as a hypothetical; we struggle to imagine that we would ever literally be asked to do this, or even to imagine that God would allow this.

Not that there are *no* costs to living your Christian faith in America. Perhaps the cost you pay is that your ability to get married is limited because you can't find a Christian to marry. Or perhaps you must make the tough decision to pull your child out of school because you want to minimize their exposure to the secular messages taught. Or maybe you miss out on some of the fun your non-Christian peers are having and instead must explain why you're not joining them in certain behaviors. Or, as I was in graduate school, you are mocked by your peers. This is a cost, and these sacrifices are real. The suffering you experience as a result is recognized by God, and he's pleased by your obedience to his commands. At the same time, we cannot equate this with true persecution, and we must consider that these prices we pay are not comparable with the kind of cost counting that takes place in countries where it is illegal to be Christian—where Christians are hunted down, jailed, and sometimes even killed.

Comparing these costs in *The Martyr's Oath*, Moore continues,

> We look with such peculiarity at the willingness of our brothers and sisters to die, and they look at us in the same way. They are totally confused that our faith costs us almost nothing—maybe 10 percent of our income and the occasional remark at work. Do we really serve the same Jesus if we're content to allow our faith to cost us so little? Here's the solution: long before our faith costs us our *life*, it has to cost us our *self*.[5]

There are Christians living today who will pay with their very lives for their commitment to their faith. While we are not faced with that same life-or-death decision, we encounter challenges every day that pit *self* against God or *self* against neighbor where we refuse to put *self* to death.

We also must consider that there are places in the world where changing your religion is socially tantamount to betraying your family, betraying your country, and betraying your identity—and that there are Christians who still choose to make this weighty sacrifice of "denying" their heritage and family to publicly declare Christ. When I shared the gospel with Muslims in China, they said they couldn't become Christians because they were already Muslim, and they were Muslim because they were of a certain ethnic background; therefore, because of their ethnic background, they couldn't be Christian. I can't imagine if someone said if you become Christian you can't be Black anymore and you are no longer welcome at Black cultural events. Most people in the US simply don't have this mindset since nearly every permutation of faith and ethnic background exists. No one would say we are denying our Americanness by converting to Christianity. In fact, it is often the non-Christian option that is seen as un-American and an attack on "American" values.

We have much to learn from our family members for whom following Christ costs them dearly. Their experiences may look a lot more like the early church than American Christianity does. Whether we recognize it or not, Christianity in the US has long enjoyed a privileged position within society. Learning from our brothers and sisters living in places where they experience persecution helps us connect with the story and culture of the Bible better. It can be challenging for us to imagine what people in the Bible went through, but when we see brothers and sisters going through it today, we have the opportunity to better understand the weight of what is being asked of us when we follow Christ.

In 2018, Christian leaders in China drafted a public statement in response to the increasing severity of government restrictions and harassment the church there faced. It was not complaint but proclamation; they were prepared to lose everything for their faith. The second of their declarations states, "Christian churches in China are eager and determined to walk the path of the cross of Christ and are more than willing to imitate the older generation of saints who suffered and were martyred for their faith."[6] They understand acutely something we only assent to in the abstract: that the way of the cross has but one terminus, and that is the cross. Not comfort or privilege.

The Promise of Persecution

When I say, "the promise of persecution," I mean two things.

First, we are forewarned that persecution and the hatred of the world will find us sooner or later if we follow Christ. Paul writes to Timothy in 2 Timothy 3:12 with such a promise: "Indeed, all who desire to live a godly life in Christ Jesus will be persecuted." This idea isn't unique to the time of the early church; Jesus had also shared a similar warning with his disciples in John 15:18-20 to prepare them for what was to come:

> If the world hates you, know that it has hated me before it hated you. If you were of the world, the world would love you as its own; but because you are not of the world, but I chose you out of the world, therefore the world hates you. Remember the word that I said to you: "A servant is not greater than his master." If they persecuted me, they will also persecute you.

To summarize, to live for Christ is to encounter persecution.

Second, despite the potential for pain, persecution also holds the potential for growth. Suffering produces endurance and hope (Romans 5:3-5) as well as steadfastness. In fact, we do not grow without steadfastness: "Let steadfastness have its full effect, that you may be perfect and complete, lacking in nothing" (James 1:4). In his commentary on James, Scottish Baptist minister Alexander MacLaren defines steadfastness as "bearing unresistingly and unmurmuring, and with the full consent of a yielding will, whatever pains, sorrows, losses, troubles, or disappointments may come into our lives, but it includes more than that…It is perseverance in the teeth of the wind, and not merely keeping our place in spite of it."[7] There's no path to perfection and completeness that does not travel through steadfastness. We cannot claim to be maturing disciples without it. Steadfastness also keeps us from being ineffective and unfruitful, and we cannot help but be nearsighted without it (1 Peter 1:8-9).

It is not a given that all those persecuted will endure—Christlikeness is both a prerequisite for persecution and its fruit. In the Parable of the Sower, the seed sown on rocky ground is received with joy but, rootless, falls away at the first sign of persecution or suffering. We can expect suffering and persecution as we pursue Christlikeness, counting the cost. We should also expect the grace to endure it.

Persecution Advances the Gospel

In Acts 16:25-32, the story of Paul and the Philippian jailer portrays Christ-followers whose priority is the gospel—even over their freedom or an end to their suffering.

> About midnight Paul and Silas were praying and singing hymns to God, and the prisoners were listening to them, and suddenly there was a great earthquake, so that the foundations of the prison were shaken. And immediately all the doors were opened, and everyone's bonds were unfastened. When the jailer woke and saw that the prison doors were open, he drew his sword and was about to kill himself, supposing that the prisoners had escaped. But Paul cried with a loud voice, "Do not harm yourself, for we are all here." And the jailer called for lights and rushed in, and trembling with fear he fell down before Paul and Silas. Then he brought them out and said, "Sirs, what must I do to be saved?" And they said, "Believe in the Lord Jesus, and you will be saved, you and your household." And they spoke the word of the Lord to him and to all who were in his house.

Paul received a clear opportunity to escape, to free himself, however temporarily, from his chains, yet he prioritized the gospel. This is the power of love for God and a deep knowledge of the goodness of the gospel. In fact, Paul was free. It was the jailer who was imprisoned on that night; Paul cared more about the work of setting the jailer free. From a jail cell, Paul also wrote these words to a church in Philippi:

> Now I want you to know, brothers and sisters, that what has
> happened to me has actually served to advance the gospel.
> As a result, it has become clear throughout the whole pal-
> ace guard and to everyone else that I am in chains for Christ.
> And because of my chains, most of the brothers and sisters
> have become confident in the Lord and dare all the more to
> proclaim the gospel without fear (Philippians 1:12-14 NIV).

Seeing Paul's boldness in the face of suffering was contagious and empowering. This is a gift we receive from watching and praying for our brothers and sisters whose faith costs them dearly. May we be made bolder!

The Church That Cried Persecution

One of the most profoundly impactful experiences I had was while singing in a worship choir at a missions conference in Southeast Asia. From the stage, I had a panoramic view of the audience singing along. Directly across from me in the first few rows were Chinese Christians getting to experience the freedom of worship for the first time. They did not have to worry about security or be self-conscious about their volume; instead, they could finally get to worship without constraints. It was not as if I had never seen arms raised during worship, but I got the chills as I witnessed their tears and jubilation. What a complete difference from my normal experience! How often I'd stood only as a formality, my mind wandering while my mouth projected words into the air I just as soon forgot. I'd get to the end of a verse without really knowing what I'd sung about. Words and choruses were so familiar I stopped appreciating their meaning. The way these Chinese Christians sang each joyful word—as though the force of their conviction could propel it up to the heavens—was like nothing I'd ever seen before.

I am not saying God prefers his church flourish under persecution rather than flourish in peace. But persecution has a sanctifying effect that isn't replicated by an unquestioned embrace of power or prefer-ential treatment. It seems scandalous or backward to say that suffering is for our good, but the Bible tells us this over and over again. We are to "rejoice in our sufferings" (Romans 5:3), for they do not compare to the glory that will be revealed in us (Romans 8:18). Ask the average American Christian what discipleship looks like and they will say quiet times, mentorship, Sunday teaching, accountability. These are good, but they aren't everything. Give them 100 chances and they probably will not come up with answers like *hardship*, *not getting my way*, or *marginalization*. We write off these difficulties as obstacles to blessed lives rather than recognize them as some of the finest possible instruments for shaping us after our beloved.

We must learn to recognize the price of faith not as waste, inconvenience, or needless pain, but as treasure. We should learn from the fortitude of our brothers and sisters in the face of life-threatening pressure to deny Christ. Learn to bear more patiently the scratches and scrapes of rising secularism. Learn to shine brightly despite the dark. Learn to trust God for the health of the church rather than the State. Learn to see that the power of the gospel is no less powerful where freedoms are not guaranteed. Learn that renewal isn't the bedfellow of state-sponsored—or even state-endorsed—faith.

In his commentary on the gospel of Matthew, Stanley Hauerwas writes,

> The shallow character of many strategies for renewal is revealed just to the extent that the resulting churches cannot understand how Christians might face persecutions. This is a particular problem in America, where Christians cannot imagine how being a Christian might put them in tension with the American way of life. This is as true for Christians on the left as it is for Christians on the right. Both mistakenly assume, often in quite similar ways, that freedom is a necessary condition for discipleship.[8]

But the testimony of persecuted Christians across time and cultures tells a different story. We *can* flourish under restricted freedoms because God is not restricted. Our most fundamental freedoms—from the law, sin, and death—mean we can weather these changes by grace with our faith and witness intact. With God's help, we can be those who conquer to the end and eat of the tree of life in paradise with God, our exceedingly great reward.

Reflection Questions

1. What are some small ways that your faith costs you something in your daily life?

   _____

   _____

   _____

   _____

2. What are your fears about the decline of Christianity in America? In what ways do you tie vibrant faith to institutional support?

   _____

   _____

   _____

   _____

3. How does the example of Christians around the world and across time—Christians whose faith was strengthened rather than weakened by persecution—encourage you? How does it challenge you?

   _____

   _____

   _____

   _____

4. How might institutional support for your faith allow you to grow complacent in your walk with Christ? In what ways might being challenged force you to grow?

   _____

   _____

   _____

   _____

5. Even in the relative comfort of present-day America, is there a cost for your faith you are hesitant to pay? How could you be a bolder or more gracious witness for Christ?

_____

_____

_____

_____

6. What views about self-preservation might be holding you back from relying on God?

_____

_____

_____

_____

12

SUFFERING AND
LAMENT

Whoever sings songs to a heavy heart
is like one who takes off a garment on a cold day,
and like vinegar on soda.

Proverbs 25:20

Moirology—a term and practice most of us are unfamiliar with. I became familiar with it through funeral scenes in historical movies and television shows. It stretches as far back into antiquity as ancient Egypt, and the Bible even references it. Amos refers to moirologists, professional mourners, as those "skilled at lamentation" (Amos 5:16), and Jeremiah requested their assistance in facilitating Israel's mourning:

> Thus says the LORD of hosts: "Consider, and call for the mourning women to come; send for the skillful women to come; let them make haste and raise a wailing over us, that our eyes may run down with tears and our eyelids flow with water" (Jeremiah 9:17-18).

Historically, moirologists—often women—provided an important service to their own communities. Today, they may be hired from outside the community to guide guests in lament or deliver eulogies at funerals. When the practice appeared in Greek tragedies, it would start with a single voice, later joined by others. One of Taiwan's few remaining moirologists spoke of the service she provides:

> This work can really help people release their anger, or help them say the things they're afraid to say out loud. For people who are afraid to cry, it helps too, because everyone cries together."[1]

Moirologists are true outsiders to the community, but by their example, they create a space where others can feel free to express their sorrow. Similarly, those who have made peace with lament as a regular part of the life of faith can be our guides when sorrow wishes to hide.

The American church, by and large, does not know how to lament. If grief can be masked, we mask it. But those who suffer well and give voice to their grief through lament can teach others its importance; they can destigmatize the sorrow, pain, and frustration each believer invariably faces in their life. Church shouldn't be a place where we show up put together, blessed and highly favored, without a care in the world. People should be able to bring their pain, week after week, without fearing others will grow weary of their hurt and dismiss them as needy, oversensitive, or one of those people for whom "there is always something." For many of us, there *is* always something, and too often, the church fails to be that hoped-for haven. Those who live with disabilities may not be given the accommodations they need to meaningfully participate in the community. Those who suffer from chronic or mental illnesses or long-term medical conditions may still be dismissed or overlooked, leaving them feeling both burdened and burdensome. Those plunged into unexpected seasons of sorrow may be met with short-term sympathy yet fail to receive ongoing support, forcing them to grieve alone in silence.

Yet God never receives those with persistent needs—which is all of us—with fatigue or diminished patience. Psalm 56:8 says, "You keep track of all my sorrows. You have collected all my tears in your bottle. You have recorded each one in your book" (NLT). God does not begrudge our tears. He sees each drop and treats them tenderly. They are neither forgotten nor tossed aside. Our care for those who suffer, however long or often, should be marked by that same tender patience.

Lament, My Friend

When I was studying in Seattle, I attended a Christian concert. At that point, I was three years into a personal "dark night of the soul," and had developed a close friendship with lament. I didn't know if lament had other friends; it felt like just the two of us. Those around me tried to explain away my sorrow and frustration or offer me "higher" spiritual fodder for thought. Yet platitudes could neither soothe my pain, nor penetrate the growing emptiness I felt. But on the evening of April 23, 2011, at Chinese Baptist Church, the lead singer put his fingers to the keys and put words to the messy reality of the despondency I had come to know as he and his band performed a song titled "Lament."

Perhaps he had wrestled with the idea of presenting himself to the world as "just fine," as we so often do—as *I* so often do. I've had seasons where, before leaving for church, I've rehearsed responses to "How are you?" that were much more cheerful and optimistic than I actually felt. Perhaps the singer had wondered about how this song—a mixture of praise and doubt and complaint—would be received; or that closing on a "maybe" as to whether this whole faith thing works out in the end might be a step too far for some.

But that evening, as his words resonated about and within me, I felt for the first time that maybe lament had other friends too. His lament was a gift to me, a crack in the surrounding darkness. It was a gift to him too. To be able to bring his full self to his worship. To not need to put a lid on his questions. To put faith and hope and sorrow to song. To show up unfinished, weaknesses unconcealed. To be honest. Unlike the joyful songs sung to my heavy heart, this one was a salve to my wounds. Through his words, God sowed in me new seeds of hope. Dawn broke on my dark night, and Seattle turned out to be my Ephraim, Joseph's second son whose name meant "God has made me fruitful in the land of my suffering."

In *Dark Clouds, Deep Mercy,* Mark Vroegop writes, "Lament is how you live between the poles of a hard life and trusting in God's sovereignty."[2] Churches that do lament well take to heart the command to mourn with those who mourn. Their leadership models vulnerability. They also are aware of who is or may be suffering. I recall often feeling lonely when something traumatic would happen in the Black community while my non-Black friends carried on with their lives completely unaware. There was no chance they'd mourn with me since they didn't even know there was anything to mourn. But as friends widened their scope of vision and received with openness my feedback about how their silence felt to me, they were able to join me as I mourned. My church, also, has begun holding lament services for different kinds of loss that create space for people to process together in community.

The Gifts Found in Suffering

Fast-forward several years after the Chinese Baptist Church concert, and weariness once again returned for a visit. I'd lost my job, and it had taken over a year to find another one. After I'd received a cascade of rejections to opportunities I'd hoped would finally provide an escape from unemployment and instability, a friend wrote to check in. I shared with him a favorite quote of mine by the seventeenth century Welsh minister Matthew Henry:

> Our earnest expectation and hope should not be to be honoured of men, or to escape the cross, but to be upheld amidst temptation, contempt, and affliction. Let us leave it to Christ, which way he will make us serviceable to his glory, whether by labour or suffering, by diligence or patience, by living to his honour in working for him, or dying to his honour in suffering for him.[3]

Let us leave it to Christ. These words had become my own. I'd learned to trust God with my situation and align my priorities with his. Above all else, my heart had begun to desire to live first to be made like Christ; I longed to become—even in unsavory circumstances—a fragrant carrier of his scent in a world prioritized differently. I'd adopted the endgame of making much of God that I might display his surpassing power. In this season, I would pray for a return to stability yet pine after serviceability to his glory. I would reject both the unquestioned embrace of smoother and easier as better and the junta rule of achievement, advancement, and stability governing my life. I would watch, as Elijah did, for signs of rain, and for grace to flower in the shadowed corners of my heart.

As I wrote to my friend, I reflected further upon three blessings that brought me comfort amid this season of difficulty. Though I had so little control over my situation, I felt encouraged knowing I still had the ability to advance the gospel regardless of my circumstances; to be made a better comforter as I received God's comfort; and to display God's power as he alone held the reins of my life. Thinking back to that time, even I cannot help but see the hand of the Spirit in allowing me to understand and appreciate these as gifts gained by trying means.

Advance the Gospel

We often talk about discerning God's will for our lives and dis-covering our callings. I'm always cautious of using the word *calling* to describe things not explicitly mentioned in the Bible, because as much as I would love to open the Bible and point to where it unequivocally says, "God promises you (fulfilling) work" or "we are called to regu-lar permanent employment," it offers no such assurances. Instead, it speaks to our uninterruptible callings—to love my neighbor and point them to Christ (if these two are not actually one and the same). What-ever else my circumstance could take from me, these they could not. No season fails to provide opportunity for their use. Paul was encour-aged, whether imprisoned or free, that he could still advance the gos-pel. His ultimate calling continued. Likewise, in loving my neighbor and pointing them to Christ amid trials, so could mine.

Be Made a Better Comforter

During that time, I was also encouraged by knowing I would grow in my ability to support others going through their own hard times. Meeting God in my sadness was its own form of ministry training. One of the Scriptures that hung over this season for me was 2 Corinthians 1:3-5: "Praise be to the God and Father of our Lord Jesus Christ, the Father of compassion and the God of all comfort, who comforts us in all our troubles, so that we can comfort those in any trouble with the comfort we ourselves receive from God. For just as we share abundantly in the sufferings of Christ, so also our comfort abounds through Christ" (NIV). Even as I struggled, I was being made into a better comforter.

Display God's Power

The Christian privilege of reflecting God is one I do not take lightly. That we are empowered to live lives that mirror the beauty and holiness of the Majestic One could never be earned. Just like my calling to advance the gospel and my enrollment in the discipleship school of suffering, I also cherished the thought that my God might be more evident to others through my circumstances. To conclude my letter to my friend, I wrote:

> Like thermochromic paint that disappears to reveal what's underneath when heated, our strength gives way to God's power when we endure hardship relying on grace. I think of Joseph and his crazy, unpredictable, pretzel-shaped life. When Joseph reveals his identity to his brothers, he says it's "not you that sent me but God" and acknowledges God as being behind all that happens. What comforts me is that I, like Joseph, will be a greater blessing because of this than I would have been otherwise, that I might somehow be able to better display God's power because of how I've endured.

Revealing God

When I finally found a permanent job, a friend threw a dinner in my honor to celebrate. Different people shared what they'd learned from observing me walk—and at times, crawl—through that stage of life. One shared the following from Timothy Keller's book on suffering: "When believers handle suffering rightly, they are not merely glorifying God to God. They are showing the world something of the greatness of God—and perhaps nothing else can reveal him to people in quite the same way."[4] Whether we realize it or not, how we suffer not only reveals to us our true beliefs about God but communicates them to an onlooking world.

During the pandemic, experts debated the effects of mask-wearing on the linguistic development of children. Some studies showed that having people's mouths covered slowed linguistic progress. This indicates that hearing people speak is not enough to learn how to speak—we must be able to watch people speak as well. This reminds me of the role discipleship plays in the process of our learning to follow Jesus: Simply listening to others speak of living for Christ is insufficient. We need to see it in action.

Whether you feel isolated and like an outsider due to the effects of physical or mental illness, financial hardship, loss, wilderness wandering, injustice, or any other trial, you can still hold the privileged position of being one "skilled at lamentation." Through the hardship you face, you can become a modeler of question asking; inviter of vulnerability; and creator of spaces where others show up unfinished, weaknesses revealed. Those skilled at lament become leaders of the chorus and enable others to join in.

Sometimes, pointing others to Christ looks like being honest about your suffering instead of trying to hide it behind a smile. By simply entering into your own pain, sweating its drops of blood, declaring "My soul is exceedingly sorrowful," and making repeated requests for friends to keep watch over you, you are demonstrating what it means to actively entrust yourself to a God who refuses to take the cup you least desire from you. Esther Fleece writes,

> Scripture doesn't tell us to pretend we are peaceful when we are not, act like everything is fine when it's not, and do everything we can to suppress our sorrow. God doesn't insist that we go to our "happy place" and ignore our sad, yet so many of our churches preach that we will have peace and prosperity just by virtue of being Christians. Scripture, in contrast, tells us that as followers of Christ, we are called to serve a "man of sorrows" who died a gruesome death. Until we identify ourselves with our Savior and acknowledge, as He did, just how painful life can be, we won't be able to lament or to overcome. And if we silence our own cries, then we will inevitably silence the cries of those around us. We cannot carefully address the wounds of others if we are carelessly addressing our own.[5]

I once worked for a highly dysfunctional organization. They hired consultants to interview staff about work culture, and when they presented their findings at the end, they pulled out a quote they claimed was representative of the prevailing sentiment they'd encountered: "We do all of our crying in private but in public put on a happy face." This analysis made me think of the church—we shouldn't face this same problem there, yet all too often, we do.

To lament with hope, we need the ability to hold in tension a great and glorious God and the direst of circumstances. In our own finite wisdom, we won't always be able to reconcile God's beauty and goodness with the world's ugliness and cruelty—yet we must still be willing to wrestle with the fact that time and chance happen to us all. I've seen all too often that people suffering hardship tend to respond in one of two ways: Either the one suffering believes they were not good enough and begins to face their suffering with shame, or they believe God was not good enough, so they add resentment to their pain. Holy lament is the space where we bring neither shame nor resentment but simply bewilderment and pain before the Lord. For some, this is seasonal; for others, it is a regular rhythm of life.

We place a higher value on the grace we receive within prosperity than the graces of wilderness and suffering. It is not that God wants to see us suffer, but when we do endure hardship, we discover new facets of grace as we find him standing ready to comfort rather than abandon us. Suffering rouses us to the reality of ourselves and God. Job 36:15 says, "He delivers the afflicted by their affliction and opens their ear by adversity." Our ears are opened by it. We don't always have to be delivered *from* suffering—sometimes, we are delivered *by* it. And our deliverance always returns us to his sanctuary.

Lament as Strength

When we bring our lament to God, we join a long lineage of those who faithfully entrusted sadness and sorrow to him. When we come before God with our grief over the brokenness of the world, we find that however much we are pained, he is pained all the more. Lament also helps us to wait faithfully on the Lord. In *Dark Clouds, Deep Mercy*, Vroegop also writes,

> Lament allows us to embrace an endurance that is not passive. Lament helps us to practice active patience. Trust looks like talking to God, sharing our complaints, seeking God's help, and then recommitting ourselves to believe in who God is and what he has done—even as the trial continues. Lament is how we endure. It is how we trust. It is how we wait…As we wait for future deliverance, our spiritual posture need not be passive. While there may be painful circumstances beyond our control, our waiting can be spiritually productive as we intentionally follow the pathway to trust.[6]

When we slow down to grieve rather than rush forward to chase happiness, lament provides us with the blessed trio of endurance, trust, and hopeful waiting. It's precisely through our waiting on God, trusting him, and enduring that we conquer in the end and finally reach our great reward. Lament equips us for this journey.

Suffering Together

As in those Greek tragedies, mourning and lament may start as a solo but should eventually be joined by a chorus in the church. In *The Common Life in the Body of Christ*, Anglican theologian Lionel Spencer Thornton writes,

> In the Body of Christ there are, strictly speaking, no private sufferings. All are shared because there is one life of the whole. Accordingly wrong done to one member is wrong done to the whole Church and therefore to Christ himself.[7]

We are one body. Suffering ought to engage the whole body in a way little else can. First Corinthians 12:26 says, "If one part suffers, every part suffers with it" (NIV). We do well rallying around celebration, but often miss the mark when we need to come together to grieve. Glenn Packiam writes, "Lament is not only for the suffering; it is for *solidarity* with the suffering. We love our neighbor when we allow their experience of pain to become the substance of our prayer. This, after all, is what Jesus did for us."[8]

Reflection Questions

1. Were you raised in an environment where weakness was an accepted part of life or something to be avoided? Today, how do you find this upbringing affecting your mindset toward suffering—both your own and that of others?

   _____

   _____

   _____

   _____

2. What does *lament* mean to you? What does it look like in the context of your church? Your family? Your personal life? Your culture?

   _____

   _____

   _____

   _____

3. What are your top priorities when you face suffering? How does the Bible inform and affirm these values you bring to navigating pain? How might it affirm the ways you feel called to change your approach?

   _____

   _____

   _____

   _____

4. What internal and external factors prevent you from sharing your sadness and sorrows with your community?

   _____

   _____

_____

_____

5. How do you respond in the face of others' sorrow? Would those around you consider you someone they can share their sadness and sorrow with? Why or why not?

_____

_____

_____

_____

13

GRIEF OVER INJUSTICE

For if you truly amend your ways and your deeds, if you truly execute justice one with another, if you do not oppress the sojourner, the fatherless, or the widow, or shed innocent blood in this place, and if you do not go after other gods to your own harm, then I will let you dwell in this place, in the land that I gave of old to your fathers forever.

JEREMIAH 7 :5 -7

G od grieves injustice; "righteousness and justice are the foundation of his throne" (Psalm 97:2). Injustice is an affront to God's kingship, a corruption of his purposes, antithetical to his holiness. God sent prophets to warn Israel to repent of their unrighteousness and choose life. Among the ways they pursued death were resting on their religious ritual laurels, practicing syncretism—the blending of religions—and being unjust. The Lord mourned not only that they reached this state but also that they were untroubled by it (Jeremiah 6:15; 8:12). The lack of repentance makes their diagnosis all the more dire.

It is lamentable that those most grieved by injustice are victims of it, second only to their Creator. Hebrews 13:3 says, "Remember...those who are mistreated as if you yourselves were suffering" (NIV). The groups the Bible frequently mentions as being vulnerable to injustice are some of the groups we've discussed earlier in this book: those who lack safety nets and access to power and influence—those experiencing poverty, the sojourner, the fatherless, and the widow. God addresses these outsider groups specifically and promises their restoration: "For the LORD your God is God of gods and Lord of lords, the great, the mighty, and the awesome God, who is not partial and takes no bribe. He executes justice for the fatherless and the widow, and loves the sojourner, giving him food and clothing" (Deuteronomy 10:17-18). His heart for these mistreated outcasts is so tender that he required in Israel's law that his people were to treat foreigners well. In the book *Christians at the Border: Immigration, the Church, and the Bible*, Old Testament scholar Daniel Carroll says,

> The first thing that stands out in Old Testament law is the remarkable contrast that can be drawn with the other law codes of the ancient Near East…The laws are numerous, and they are gracious to the sojourner.[1]

Even so, God's people's hearts for those who suffer injustice are not always aligned with his own. Too often, the unaffected seem infinitely more interested in rationalizing, justifying, or explaining away others' pain; after all, it's easy to be apathetic about injustice when it doesn't affect us or those we hold dear. In many situations, we don't even notice injustice when it occurs because it is so far removed from our own experience; when we are finally made aware of it, we usually have the news to thank. But when we rely on the news cycle to generate and sustain our interest in injustice, it inevitably ebbs and flows; we find ourselves waiting for evil to expose itself for our public condemnation, only to wrongfully allow it to retreat behind the scenes to wreak further havoc as we do nothing to stop it.

But woe to us if our hearts grow cold with indifference when they ought to burn with righteous anger. Grief over injustice must be more than reactionary advocacy. Neither the news cycle nor personal experience should be the primary driver of our concern about injustice. Grief over injustice does more than sit back and ask to be educated. When we grieve injustice, we must work to get ahead of it. We must be open to examining our hearts and lives for its influence and our complicity. Our grief cannot be seasonal, superficial, or limited to expressions of sympathy. Grief over injustice intercedes, pleads, and refuses to be stifled.

But even in our zeal for justice, we must remain cautious; we may still suffer from favoritism or tribalism, caring only about certain kinds of injustice and not others, or only caring about forms that affect us and our community while openly condoning others. Both apathy and myopia fall short.

A Biblical View of Justice

The Bible is anything but silent on justice. Each major section of Scripture includes examples of what it is, how God administers it, and how he expects his justness to be embodied in his people. When the Bible speaks of justice, laws, leaders, and interpersonal relationships all fall within its scope. It is an immutable aspect of God's character and kingship and extends to the domain of earthly leaders. God does not pervert justice, so when we do—whether through our laws, leaders, or interpersonal relationships—we distort his image.

Because God hates injustice, he instituted judges and other civic leaders, not for them to amass riches or prestige for themselves, but for the implementation of his righteous will among his people. The scope of their power had less to do with self-aggrandizement and empire-building, than administering and securing justice for those to whom it was owed. Leadership and power held by individuals are not ends in themselves, but rather, means employed toward the ends of establishing justice and righteousness among humankind.

Biblical justice addresses injustices such as convicting the innocent and absolving the guilty. Proverbs 17:15 says, "He who justifies the wicked and he who condemns the righteous are both alike an abomination to the Lord."

On a personal level, justice is presented as something we can either love or hate, with little middle ground, and those who observe it are blessed (Psalm 106:3). God prefers justice to such religious rituals as sacrifice (Proverbs 21:3) and even fasting (Isaiah 58). It was so important, in fact, that without justice, Israel could not be considered faithful to God's covenant nor continue to receive covenant benefits. God was willing to withhold or revoke the ultimate blessing of dwelling safely in the land he intended for them to inherit for failure in this area. Deuteronomy 16:20 says, "Justice, and only justice, you shall follow, that you may live and inherit the land that the LORD your God is giving you." From God's perspective, justice—something so foundational to his identity—could not be an optional feature of his people.

God has special concern for those most vulnerable to injustice— the fatherless, weak, needy, afflicted, destitute, poor, and sojourning. Since justice is meant to be the antidote to oppression and partiality, when justice works as it should, it keeps such people safe and cared for because those who love justice would neither withhold charity from the vulnerable nor oppress others for personal gain (Proverbs 22:16; Malachi 3:5). The Bible does not portray those as unconcerned with justice neutrally, but calls them evil and says they do not seek the Lord (Proverbs 28:5).

Justice extends to issues such as using false weights and measures. Leviticus 19:35-36 says,

> You shall do no wrong in judgment, in measures of length or weight or quantity. You shall have just balances, just weights, a just ephah, and a just hin: I am the LORD your God, who brought you out of the land of Egypt.

This included cheating others in matters of commerce but also applied to employing double standards in any other area of life— even in the law itself.

Sometimes injustice is deliberate, resulting from the abuse of power, an all-consuming desire for personal gain (1 Samuel 8:3), selfishness, greed, pride, or favoritism. Other times, it may be more passive, resulting from neglect or ignorance, such as unknowingly participating in systems that oppress or mistreat vulnerable populations. Yet even when we are unintentionally unjust, we do not get a pass. Leviticus 4 and 5 discuss a range of sins committed unbeknownst to the person committing them and the sacrificial offerings required once they are made aware. Leviticus 5:17-19 (emphasis mine) summarizes the section well:

> If anyone sins, doing any of the things that by the LORD's commandments ought not to be done, *though he did not know it,* then realizes his guilt, he shall bear his iniquity. He shall bring to the priest a ram without blemish out of the flock, or its equivalent, for a guilt offering, and *the priest shall make atonement for him for the mistake that he made unintentionally,* and he shall be forgiven. It is a guilt offering; *he has indeed incurred guilt* before the LORD.

Injustice manifests itself as inequitable treatment, curtailed freedoms, restricted access to power, dignity denied, and exclusion.

Because justice is so sweeping, it has never sat well with me to limit the idea or application of justice to a single issue. No matter how important any individual issue is, prioritizing it to the exclusion of others results in overlooking other problems that help us make sense of our larger reality. Jesus isn't concerned with remedying just one kind of injustice. His interest in injustice is broad—which means our interest in justice must be broad too. Jesus talks about the poor, people with disabilities and long-term illnesses, the unjustly imprisoned, and those without legal and social protections, like widows and foreigners. Justice isn't limited, and we should be careful not to focus on one aspect of it, lest we lose sight of the whole. Founder of the Justice Conference, Ken Wytsma, describes justice this way:

> Justice is like a mosaic. It's not only about single pieces—it's also about all the pieces working together in a stunning whole. All too often we believe that our desire to pursue

justice can only be lived out or understood in a single shard. Criminal justice. International development. Creation care. Education. Anti-trafficking. Works of mercy and love. All of these shards are vital parts of God's mosaic of justice. Many of us want to pursue justice. Even if we don't understand justice as a whole, even if we are thrown for a loop by the words social justice, we want specific injustices to be rectified. So we pursue a single cause, which is wonderful...unless we allow that to be the sum total of our engagement and understanding. I may volunteer to help homeless veterans, and you may send money to build a well in Africa, in lieu of birthday presents. But if we let those good, necessary things become sufficient for understanding justice, we're neglecting far too much.

When we think a single shard of the mosaic of justice describes the whole, it's as if we're cataloging one particular butterfly and assuming we've understood every other species that swoops and sways through the sky.[2]

The Dangers of a Justice-Neutral Heart

God's heart toward justice is anything but neutral. When our own hearts are neutral, we are out of sync with what pleases God. When we do not concern ourselves with justice, we neglect our souls.

Isaiah 58 gives us a good picture of the consequences of a justice-neutral heart. Here, Isaiah addresses Israel's fasting practices. We read that certain Israelites question God while also appearing to fast correctly. They seek him daily, finding God's laws not a chore but a delight, and they want to draw near to him and seek him for righteous judgments, yet they get no commendation from him. Confused, they press God on why he appears to not acknowledge their efforts only to be called out for sins of omission. God responds to them,

> Is not this the kind of fasting I have chosen: to loose the chains of injustice and untie the cords of the yoke, to set the oppressed free and break every yoke? Is it not to share

your food with the hungry and to provide the poor wan-
derer with shelter—when you see the naked, to clothe
them, and not to turn away from your own flesh and blood
(Isaiah 58:6-7 NIV)?

Loose, undo, let free, break—all these verbs deal with freedom. Yoke,
a symbol of oppression, is repeated twice. To fast properly, then, one
must also seek freedom for the enslaved and relief for the oppressed. In
his commentary on the book of Isaiah, German Old Testament scholar
Claus Westermann asserts that,

> Helping to restore a person's freedom is more pleasing to
> God than the practice of mortifying one's flesh. This is the
> beginning of that great change which declared, in God's
> name, that men and women are of greater importance than
> cultic rites directed towards himself.[3]

God continues his response:

> If you pour yourself out for the hungry and satisfy the
> desire of the afflicted, then shall your light rise in the dark-
> ness and your gloom be as the noonday. And the LORD will
> guide you continually and satisfy your desire in scorched
> places and make your bones strong; and you shall be like
> a watered garden, like a spring of water, whose waters do
> not fail (Isaiah 58:10-11).

Watered garden? Haven't we seen this imagery before?

The garden imagery from the second half of verse 11 is also found in
Jeremiah 17 (referenced in chapter seven's discussion of trust) as well as
in Psalm 1. In Isaiah, we read that the person who fasts in this fashion
will share fates with the one who trusts the Lord. Just as the righteous
of Psalm 1 is "planted by streams of water that yields its fruit in its season, and its leaf does not wither" (Psalm 1:3) and the one who trusts
in the Lord in Jeremiah is like a "tree planted by water, that sends out
its roots by the stream, and does not fear when heat comes," and that

"does not cease to bear fruit" (Jeremiah 17:8), so is the person who seeks to undo oppression in all its guises and invests themselves fully in the plight of the vulnerable.

The release of captives and unburdening of the oppressed is the Lord's work, and we participate with him when we do the same. Jesus quotes Isaiah in Luke 4:18 to speak of his work: "The Spirit of the Lord is on me, because he has anointed me to proclaim good news to the poor. He has sent me to proclaim freedom for the prisoners and recovery of sight for the blind, to set the oppressed free" (NIV). This is the work of the true fast. And just as the humility of God was demonstrated in his close association with the most vulnerable and under-resourced throughout his incarnate life on earth, so will his children's.

The Gift of Grief over Injustice

Now that I have explained the biblical view of justice and what God requires of us, I hope it is easier to understand why grief over injustice is a gift. A heart unmoved by injustice is a heart severely out of touch with the heart of God. Nothing good ever came of Israel's disregard for justice, and nothing good will come of ours either. When apathy and ignorance toward injustice reign, we should receive this as the ringing of an alarm. This is not health. This is a community that must be warned.

The book of Isaiah opens by detailing how the southern kingdom of Judah has gone astray. God has grown sick of their religious ceremony and special festivals, their raised hands, and many prayers, offered in place of the sincere pursuit of justice and righteousness. If this were a report card, Judah would be failing. Yet even at this point before exile, they could return to God and his ways and be spared. Among the advice God gives Judah to turn things around before the final grade is issued is this: "Wash yourselves; make yourselves clean; remove the evil of your deeds from before my eyes; cease to do evil, learn to do good; seek justice, correct oppression; bring justice to the fatherless, plead the widow's cause" (Isaiah 1:16-17). Justice runs straight through these instructions. The stench of their injustice has reached the Lord, and he will tolerate it no more. Their oppression will kill them, strip them of their land, and bring them misery upon misery.

Later, from exile, Ezekiel rebukes them as well for having had so much yet giving so little and for living lives of comfort: "Behold, this was the guilt of your sister Sodom: she and her daughters had pride, excess of food, and prosperous ease, but did not aid the poor and needy" (Ezekiel 16:49). Two verses earlier, Ezekiel had accused them of being even worse than Sodom: "You were more corrupt than they in all your ways...you have made your sisters appear righteous" (Ezekiel 16:47, 52). They were so much more proud, extravagant, complacent, yet less committed to justice, that they made Sodom look good. This is quite the indictment.

In the New Testament, James—in harmony with the prophets—connects the purity of religion with practicing justice. "Religion that is pure and undefiled before God the Father is this: to visit orphans and widows in their affliction, and to keep oneself unstained from the world" (James 1:27). In his commentary on James, Scot McKnight writes,

> For James, to be pure means to be marked off in worldview from those who are unjust, oppressive, and worldly..."Pure and undefiled" are purity terms to describe the condition of a person and his or her aptness to live in the Land.[4]

If we think we can be soft toward injustice or get by with burying our heads in the sand, the Bible says otherwise. For Israel, injustice was the path toward death instead of life, toward covenant curses instead of blessings. It was partly to blame for Israel's eventual exile. We can take heed at these warnings and ask God to reshape our hearts where we are prone to indifference. To grieve injustice is anything but unorthodox; it is obedience to God and a vital, lifesaving, covenant-honoring gift to its community wherever it is found.

Recognizing All Sorts of Injustice

Grief over injustice must go beyond having a pet issue or even a personal cause. I realized several years ago that if I was exclusively interested in justice for Black Americans while being indifferent to everything else, then it was not true justice I loved, but my own comfort and freedom. If I really loved justice, I would be prepared to work toward it even when it disadvantaged me. Why? Because otherwise justice stalls. Because this is what Jesus modeled. Because this attitude is what I long to see from those who benefit from the injustices committed against me.

In the same vein, it's important that the church be a space for all sorts of people who grieve all sorts of injustices. Even while we grieve injustice, we tend to prioritize our own interests and self-preservation. But by gathering a variety of people who grieve injustice in its various forms, our picture of the scope of injustice is broadened. I recommend learning about injustices that affect communities to which you do not belong. I became much more aware of the issues and types of discrimination Asian Americans faced while attending church alongside them for three years and watching them lament, advocate for, and rally behind initiatives that would protect their community.

Injustice is broad, yet our goal is not to see it everywhere—rather, we must seek to prayerfully and humbly identify injustice and have an accurate, robust understanding of what it entails. It is good, right, and pleasing to God for us to turn over every corner of our hearts and lives looking for sin, just as Israel turned their house over in search of the smallest sign of leaven (Exodus 13:7). In Psalm 19:12, David confesses he cannot see the full scope of his faults. But Psalm 90:8 shares a remedy by acknowledging we have secret sins that only the light of God's presence can reveal. In Psalm 139:23, we find the psalmist asking God to search him. None of these verses are specifically in reference to searching for injustice, but there's no reason injustice should be excluded from their application, either, since injustice is sin.

Outsiders can help us make this identification. They can function in some ways as the prophets did, raising warnings and speaking of the need for change—hopefully, with better outcomes than the prophets received. Warnings are blessings; those who issue them are a means of grace. The one who grieves injustice within their church congregation not only helps the congregation to identify and address injustice within the church, but within their surrounding community as well. They can also help to identify ways that the church can be more proactively involved in helping to reduce injustice. Hebrews 11:32-33 says, "What more shall I say? For time would fail me to tell of Gideon, Barak, Samson, Jephthah, of David and Samuel and the prophets—who through faith conquered kingdoms, enforced justice, obtained promises, stopped the mouths of lions." Listed in the great hall of faith are those who, by faith, enforced justice. These are people worth emulating.

It's not just about the benefit that will inevitably extend to others—because Christlikeness benefits others—but grief over injustice is a part of our sanctification. Grief over injustice makes *us* like Christ. And *we* benefit from Christlikeness.

I challenge you. Set up a Google alert for injustice and set the alert so you get a daily email of the results. When you get your email, before trying to rationalize if something meets your injustice standard or not, pray for those involved: that where there are victims they'd receive justice; that the people in power would administer true justice; and that those on the sidelines would advocate as they are able for justice. Just these three things. Then to close out your prayer, ask God to make you more sensitive to injustice wherever it occurs—to show you what you can do to advocate and where he might have you focus your efforts.

Reflection Questions

1. What types of injustice have you suffered in the past? What were your takeaways from these difficult experiences?

   _____

   _____

   _____

   _____

2. What types of injustices have you committed or condoned in the past? What types of injustices might you still be committing against others today? How can you move forward in God's forgiveness and freedom from these past sins?

   _____

   _____

   _____

   _____

3. What are some steps you think it would be beneficial for you to take to make you more aware of injustice in the world?

   _____

   _____

   _____

   _____

4. How would you describe your attitude toward the concept of injustice today? When you think about the concept, do you immediately feel suspicious? Anxious? Self-righteous? Burned-out? Apathetic?

   _____

   _____

   _____

   _____

5. If God sent some of his Old Testament prophets to address the United States today, what parts of our culture do you think they would point out as unjust?

_____

_____

_____

_____

6. Grief over injustice can be heavy, so how do you currently share this burden with other people? How do you share this burden with God? How might he be calling you to better share the burdens of others as you come alongside them?

_____

_____

_____

_____

7. Read Revelation 21:1-5. How does this passage give you hope as you grieve?

_____

_____

_____

_____

8. Read Leviticus 4:13-15. What does this passage reveal about the severity of unintentional sin and the corporate nature of sin?

_____

_____

_____

_____

9. How can your church help address injustices in your community? How can your family help? In what specific ways can you person- ally help?

_____

_____

_____

_____

14

BECOMING THE CHURCH OF THE OUTSIDER

*The parts of the body that seem to be
weaker are indispensable.*

1 CORINTHIANS 12:22

We need each other.

The eye cannot say to the hand, "I have no need of you," nor again the head to the feet, "I have no need of you." On the contrary, the parts of the body that seem to be weaker are indispensable, and on those parts of the body that we think less honorable we bestow the greater honor, and our unpresentable parts are treated with greater modesty, which our more presentable parts do not require. But God has so composed the body, giving greater honor to the part that lacked it, that there may be no division in the body, but that the members may have the same care for one another. If one member suffers, all suffer together; if one member is honored, all rejoice together (1 Corinthians 12:21-26).

Regardless of our physical or ideological distance from each other, or the different roles we play within our churches or communities, we need each other. Like the eye and hand in the Scripture mentioned, you might also harbor misguided opinions about other parts of the body that lead you astray from God's design: *Because they don't function like I do, they are less important. Because they have different gifts than I do, they don't matter as much.* But the picture Paul gives of the body of Christ means missing or injured parts equals broken whole. We are vital to each other's health.

Paul's words also reveal that what we consider honorable does not always align with God's estimation. God searches out the places where people are *not* honored and bestows them with honor. He does this not to cause division, but to erase it. It's clear that it's not difference itself that creates division, but the arbitrary assignment of honor within its ranks. These errant assignments of honor likely correspond to perceived functional value as defined by the world. From God's perspective, each member of his body has been carefully placed and deliberately gifted. He breaks down divisions to make way for mutual concern, but not by removing the "weak links." Instead, God addresses the inequalities with honor. Perhaps we might attempt to mend divisions by trying the same: finding the places where people are not honored and then honoring them as God would.

No Trivial Pursuit

Scripture frequently portrays God as the ultimate beneficiary of our love toward our neighbor. In the Colossians passage on servants and masters, we read, "Whatever you do, work heartily, as for the Lord and not for men…You are serving the Lord Christ" (Colossians 3:23-24). In Proverbs 19:17, we learn, "Whoever is generous to the poor lends to the LORD." And in the well-known "least of these" passage in Matthew, Jesus reveals that he is the true recipient of the kindness and regard shown the outcast by the inheritors of his kingdom:

Then the King will say to those on his right, "Come, you who are blessed by my Father, inherit the kingdom prepared for you from the foundation of the world. For I was hungry and you gave me food, I was thirsty and you gave me drink, I was a stranger and you welcomed me, I was naked and you clothed me, I was sick and you visited me, I was in prison and you came to me." Then the righteous will answer him, saying, "Lord, when did we see you hungry and feed you, or thirsty and give you drink? And when did we see you a stranger and welcome you, or naked and clothe you? And when did we see you sick or in prison and visit you?" And the King will answer them, "Truly, I say to you, as you did it to one of the least of these my brothers, you did it to me" (Matthew 25:34-40).

Scripture also points to God as the ultimate victim of our disobedience. When God's people demand a king for Israel in 1 Samuel 8:7, God tells Samuel they aren't rejecting the prophet but God himself. When Joseph turns down Potiphar's wife's advances in Genesis 39:9, he recognizes this act of infidelity would not only dishonor Potiphar, but God himself: "How then can I do this great wickedness and sin against God?" In Psalm 51:4, David confesses, "Against you, you only, have I sinned." Proverbs 14:31 reminds us that, "Whoever oppresses a poor man insults his Maker."

Whether good or bad, God sees how we treat the outsider—in action, word, thought, or disposition of our heart—as how we treat him. When we treat them well, God is honored. When we treat them poorly, we mistreat him. When we cannot be bothered to take up their burdens, learn from them, or build community with them, pride has us in its grasp. We become like that bald mountain range described in this book's first chapter, the one that dares to say to the mountain range covered with trees, "You cannot compare with me."

When Christians treat the parts of Christ's body that appear weaker as dispensable, they distort God's design—in other words, they sin against God. To mistreat the body is a perversion of God's will. Christians who do not recognize this fall short of the obedience God calls them to and use faulty weights and measures to assess their hearts and each other. They reject truth for a lie. They become polluted by worldly thinking and open themselves to further sin. We can try to sanitize the gravity of failing to recognize the value of those who aren't like us, but this is what it is.

Outsiders bear the image of God. Insiders and outsiders in the church share a common citizenship. Ephesians 4:4-6 says, "There is one body and one Spirit—just as you were called to the one hope that belongs to your call—one Lord, one faith, one baptism, one God and Father of all, who is over all and through all and in all." The outsiders' imago Dei and citizenship in God's kingdom should suffice for others to extend a warm welcome as valued members of the community. The church is weaker when it dismisses or neglects outsiders' experiences and concerns but is made stronger and fuller when outsiders are considered and embraced.

False Starts

I once participated with my friends in a *Mario Kart* competition of losers. All of us people who always came in last played each other to see who was truly the worst. I played one whole match looking at the wrong quadrant of the screen, meaning my steering did not line up with where I wanted to go or where I thought I was going. What I was *really* doing was jamming my car into a wall in the wrong direction with gusto. For the whole game I thought I was winning, all the way until I got to the end and realized I was in last place.

This can easily happen with us. We think we're winning, but we've long been going in reverse with gusto. That's why our endgame matters. I was not looking in the right place, so not only did I fail to reach my destination, but I went nowhere for the duration of the match.

When we live in silos and echo chambers, we construct worlds for ourselves void of the very road signs that might otherwise tell us we're going the wrong way. In all of our thoughts about God, we think our group alone is sufficient in itself for understanding how wide, how long, how high, and how deep the love of Christ and the grandeur of his design. Our group is sufficient for reflecting who he is. This is nothing but pride.

One year for Halloween, I dressed up as the Token Black Friend for a friend's party. My outfit was simple: I just grabbed something from my closet, double-checked the guest list, and showed up as I was. I got a kick out of people trying to figure out what I was in my belted black maxi dress. I even put some coins in my pocket to jingle in case anyone needed a hint. Making things awkward is my cardio.

Tokenism is not embracing diversity.

To become the church of the outsider, we cannot be satisfied by simply putting out extra chairs for "others." There are right and wrong ways to go about becoming a church that welcomes outsiders. Adding leaves to tables is not enough. In fact, without preparing the hearts of insiders, those extra leaves may do outsiders more harm than good. The focus shouldn't be on the quantity of outsiders but on the quality of relationships being built with them. Reducing token diversity members to their most superficial difference fails to see them as whole or recognize their multidimensionality and innate value.

One of the dangers in a church working to diversify its community lies in the risk of approaching outsiders as projects. Another lies in commodifying people with diverse backgrounds based on the perspective you want them to offer. It's true that people with disabilities and chronic illness can provide a valuable perspective on those experiences, but they have so much more to offer than that. Racial minorities can speak to race, but they, too, are complex human beings who should be recognized and valued simply because they are fellow image-bearers of God, whether they want to engage the topic of race or not. Projecting your assumptions about the potential contributions of others fails to see them as multidimensional people with varied gifts and perspectives.

The Adapted, Adapting, and Unadapted

What often happens in Christian spaces is that there is a dominant group that has set the culture. They can be considered fully adapted. The outsiders among them fall into one of two categories: those attempting to adapt to the prevailing culture (the adapting) and those utterly foreign to the inside culture (the unadapted).

It's not uncommon for churches to point to the outsiders who have traveled the spectrum from unadapted to fully or mostly adapted and say, "Success!" They rarely have to confront the number of people who are unadapted because most of them don't stick around long. They also don't think to look at all the insiders who started out as adapted to measure how far they've ventured into the "adapting" group to meet the outsider where they are—yet this distance matters.

A culture of conceit forces all outsiders to participate on the insider's terms and meet the insider where they are. We err when we believe that having outsiders adapt to the dominant culture must always be our goal. What delights the heart of God is when the adapted become the adapting so they can ease the burden of the unadapted. Is this not what it means to consider others as more significant than yourself (Philippians 2:3)? To "bear one another's burdens, and so fulfill the law of Christ" (Galatians 6:2)? To submit to one another "out of reverence for Christ" (Ephesians 5:21)?

Paul writes to the church in Rome, "We who are strong have an obligation to bear with the failings of the weak, and not to please ourselves" (Romans 15:1). But who are the strong? And who are the weak? Sometimes it is the outsiders who must bear with the failings of the insiders. Practicing favoritism is a weakness. Low tolerance for discomfort is a weakness. Those with privilege who've never done anything with it but hoard and deny it? Those obsessed with defending their own personal rights and ensuring they get what they believe is their fair share? Those who narrowly define vulnerability, who uphold only strength as strength and believe weakness can only be weakness? These people all find themselves in a place of weakness.

But the ones still radiating Christ despite their circumstances and showing the rest of us what lives of deep faith can look like? Those are the powerhouse strong who must bear with the rest of us. These are the ones leading the pack. These are the most spiritually fit when it comes to God's kingdom.

By God's grace, we are made better by living faithfully on the outside. We become stronger comforters, givers, justice-seekers, demonstrators of God's power, and followers of Christ—wherever he may lead. We ourselves benefit from the graces of suffering, dependence, freedom, perspective, empathy, and love for God both by possessing them and being a witness to the power of Christ.

Members of One Body

Paul adopts the body politic imagery for the church and then subverts it. The original intent was that the weak should be accommodating of the strong to achieve unity, but in Paul's version, the strong must be willing to take the interests of the weak into consideration. He turned on its head a principle active in the culture that did nothing to elevate or honor the lowest socially ranked individuals so that they are deferred to and honored. In *Uncomfortable: The Awkward and Essential Challenge of Christian Community*, Brett McCracken writes, "But if the church is to thrive in the twenty-first century, she must recover the jarring and profound paradoxes of what Christ calls her to embody: a kingdom where last is first, giving is receiving, dying is living, losing is finding, least is greatest, poor is rich, weakness is strength, serving is ruling."[1] These profound paradoxes challenge us to live beyond our nature and divest from the values of the culture. It is a kingdom of outsiders.

In the first chapter, I said that the story of the Bible was a story about nothings and that today, God still chooses and transforms nothings. Chosen while yet sinners, we live to be made like Christ, the ultimate outsider, who dispensed with the glory and comforts of heaven to give himself, a treasure of matchless worth, to rebels and riffraff. He was rich, yet for our sake became poor that we might become rich (2 Corinthians 8:9). Trusting the Father, he spoke the life-saving promise, "Nevertheless, not my will, but yours, be done" (Luke 22:42), that we might trust him and be brought near. This is our better boast.

A Church for Outsiders

So, what does a diverse community of self-mortifying, neighbor-edifying, right-forfeiting, enemy-blessing heirs of grace look like?

In a community where vision is appreciated, majority members have the humility to listen to the insights outsiders may have about internal culture. Fringe concerns are recognized as everyone's concern. We reflect soberly upon ourselves and seek input on how we can repent of culturally acceptable sins. Challenges to the status quo are received as opportunities to grow. Individuals are open about their weaknesses.

Where interdependence is valued, our neediness connects us to each other and to God without shame. We recognize our limits and carry each other's burdens. We trust God with our loneliness and take seriously our sacred mission of undistracted adoration. If we have families, we welcome in singles.

When we value true freedom—rather than just *personal* freedom—we refuse to let power, comfort, or greed corrupt ourselves or our communities. Our freedom in Christ is tied to the good of our neighbor (1 Corinthians 10:31-33). We also learn to exercise our discomfort muscles to better ensure the weight of discomfort is evenly distributed. We look to God when we feel powerless; if we have power, we steward it so as many people can benefit from it as possible.

What connects us as Christ-followers is more binding than what separates us. When empathy is valued, we can mourn with those who mourn and rejoice with those who rejoice. When perspective is valued, we have the full mosaic of gifts and experiences at our disposal for use in the church. Different perspectives expose us to a wider array of existing realities and expand our collective imagination.

While not exhaustive, the following suggestions can aid communities in becoming the kinds of spaces where those on the outside can flourish. These graces make our hearts "outsider ready." Kind of like winterizing your car, having a heart prepared to care well and adjust for the outsider is good for insider and outsider alike. If you don't prepare in advance, when the time to get on the road comes, things may not work out as you'd hoped. For a commitment to outsiders to go beyond performative or short-lived trends, we must seek God earnestly and persistently for the grace to change and the humility to learn from those already leading the way. We can

- grow in trust
- maintain proper perspective on the source and ends of God's blessings
- develop for ourselves and our communities the grace of liberality
- share the burden of discomfort with others
- educate ourselves on the experiences and needs of different marginalized groups
- prepare for persecution through little daily deaths
- cry when we need to cry
- honor our limits
- uplift the unmarried and welcome them into our homes
- grieve injustice
- recognize our interdependence
- reject self-sufficiency
- get outside our comfort zones
- question our hearts
- live humbly and curiously
- root our identities and futures in God

Christ was the consummate insider who became an outsider for us. And before departing, he left us this encouragement: "Truly, truly, I say to you, whoever believes in me will also do the works that I do; and greater works than these will he do, because I am going to the Father" (John 14:12).

Friends, we can do greater works because Jesus went to the Father and there remains interceding for us. Let us wear him out for the grace to be faithful undivided insiders and outsiders with affection and mutual care for one another. Let us trust, stretch, adore, depend, give, endure, suffer, and seek justice out of reverence for Christ, who trusted, stooped down, loved, depended, gave, suffered, and endured for our eternal good.

Reflection Questions

1. Think about a time when you were an outsider. What did that feel like, and how did you respond?

    _____

    _____

    _____

    _____

2. What rhythms can you build into your life to encourage a deeper sense of humility? What about compassion, empathy, or anything else that might help you better serve others?

    _____

    _____

    _____

    _____

3. How do you most frequently find yourself comparing yourself with others in the church?

    _____

    _____

    _____

    _____

4. Read 1 Corinthians 1:27-33. What do you think the difference is between true freedom and personal freedom?

    _____

    _____

    _____

    _____

5. Among the profound paradoxes from Brett McCracken's list from
   *Uncomfortable: The Awkward and Essential Challenge of Christian
   Community*, which of these is hardest for you to imagine or live
   out?

   _____

   _____

   _____

   _____

NOTES

Introduction

1. *The Shorter Catechism*, Orthodox Presbyterian Church, https://www.opc.org/documents/SCLayout.pdf.

Chapter 1—Who Is an Outsider?

1. Robert Kelsey, *The Outside Edge: How Outsiders Can Succeed in a World Made by Insiders* (Chichester, West Sussex: Wiley, 2015), 13.

2. Charles Hodge, *Commentary on the First Epistle to the Corinthians* (Grand Rapids, MI: Eerdmans Publishing Company, 1994), 25.

3. Dietrich Bonhoeffer, *Life Together* (Minneapolis, MN: Fortress Press, 2015), 7.

4. Anthony C. Thiselton, *1 Corinthians: A Shorter Exegetical & Pastoral Commentary* (Grand Rapids, MI: Eerdmans Publishing Co., 2006), 208-209.

5. David E. Garland, *1 Corinthians (Baker Exegetical Commentary on the New Testament)* (Ada, MI: Baker Publishing Group, 2003), 41.

Chapter 2—Vision: Seeing the Inside

1. David Foster Wallace, "This is Water," *Farnam Street* (blog), https://fs.blog/david-foster-wallace-this-is-water.

2. David P. Nystrom, *James* (Grand Rapids, MI: Zondervan, 1997), 180.

Chapter 3—Perspective: Seeing from Your Experience

1. Lisa McKay, "Disabilities, Differences, and Diversity: A Reflection on Parenting a Child with 'Dis-Abilities,'" *Lisa McKay Writing* (blog), September 23, 2022, https://www.lisamckaywriting.com/disability-differences-diversity-parenting-a-child.

2. Anthony C. Thiselton, *1 Corinthians: A Shorter Exegetical & Pastoral Commentary* (Grand Rapids, MI: Eerdmans Publishing Company, 2006), 212.

3. Mark DeYmaz, *Ethnic Blends: Mixing Diversity into Your Local Church* (Grand Rapids, MI: Zondervan, 2010), 99.

4. Amy Kenny, *My Body Is Not a Prayer Request: Disability Justice in the Church* (Grand Rapids, MI: Brazos Press, 2022), 111.

5. Roy E. Ciampa and Brian S. Rosner, *The First Letter to the Corinthians* (Grand Rapids, MI: W.B. Eerdmans, 2010), 94.

6. David Rock and Heidi Grant, "Why Diverse Teams Are Smarter," *Harvard Business Review*, November 4, 2016, https://hbr.org/2016/11/why-diverse-teams-are-smarter.

Chapter 4—Empathy: Seeing Others' Pain

1. Lois Lowry, *The Giver* (Boston, MA: Houghton Mifflin Harcourt, 1993), 5-6.

2. Frank Dikötter, *The Construction of Racial Identities in China and Japan Historical and Contemporary Perspectives* (Hong Kong: Hong Kong University Press, 1997), 9.

3. Olivia Goldhill, "Empathy makes us immoral, says a Yale psychologist," *Quartz*, July 9, 2017, https://qz.com/1024303/empathy-makes-us-immoral-says-a-yale-psychologist.

4. David N. Perkins and Gavriel Salomon, "Transfer of Learning," Contribution to the *International Encyclopedia of Education, Second Edition* (Oxford: Pergamon Press, 1992), https://openlab.citytech.cuny.edu/fywpd/files/2020/01/transferoflearning.pdf.

5. Humans of New York, "I'm aware of it all day, every day. We're triggered all the time, even the best of us," Facebook, September 23, 2022, https://www.facebook.com/humansofnewyork/posts/8472790232795002.

6. Gareth Lee Cockerill, *The Epistle to the Hebrews* (Grand Rapids, MI: Eerdmans Publishing Company, 2012), 225.

7. R. Kent Hughes, *Hebrews (Vol. 1): An Anchor for the Soul* (Wheaton, IL: Crossway, 2015), 177.

Chapter 5—Lack and Limits: A Grace-Filled Awareness of Need

1. Edward T. Welch, *Side by Side: Walking with Others in Wisdom and Love* (Wheaton, IL: Crossway, 2015), 13.

2. Lyndsey Medford (@lyndseymedford), "Notes from the days of moving with a chronic illness," Instagram, September 12, 2022, https://www.instagram.com/p/CibSzBhOIqk.

3. Craig L. Blomberg, *Christians in an Age of Wealth: A Biblical Theology of Stewardship* (Grand Rapids, MI: Zondervan Academic, 2013), 69-70.

4. Amy Kenny, *My Body Is Not a Prayer Request: Disability Justice in the Church* (Grand Rapids, MI: Brazos Press, 2022), 112.

5. A. Andrews, "As a disabled person, I know: American bootstrap culture is a lie," *Washington Post*, September 11, 2022, https://www.washingtonpost.com/lifestyle/2022/09/11/disabled-person-i-know-american-bootstrap-culture-is-lie.

6. Jen Oshman, "Girl, Follow Jesus," *Gospel Coalition*, March 4, 2019, https://www.thegospelcoalition.org/reviews/girl-stop-apologizing.

7. Stanley Hauerwas, *Matthew (Brazos Theological Commentary on the Bible)* (Grand Rapids, MI: Brazos Publishing Co., 2015), 203.

8. David L. Turner and Darrel L. Bock, *Cornerstone Biblical Commentary: The Gospel of Matthew; The Gospel of Mark*, ed. Philip W. Comfort (Carol Stream, IL: Tyndale House Publishers, 2005), 186.

9. Randy Alcorn, *Money, Possessions, and Eternity* (Carol Stream, IL: Tyndale House, 2003), 64.

10. Peter Scazzero, *Emotionally Healthy Discipleship: Moving from Shallow Christianity to Deep Transformation* (Grand Rapids, MI: Zondervan, 2021), 96.

Chapter 6—Devotion: The Gift of Singleness

1. Sam Allberry, *7 Myths About Singleness* (Wheaton, IL: Crossway, 2019), 37.

2. Dan B. Allender and Tremper Longman III, *Breaking the Idols of Your Heart: How to Navigate the Temptations of Life* (Downers Grove, IL: InterVarsity Press, 2009), 54.

Chapter 7—Trust: When You Can't Believe What You See

1. Sovereign Grace Christian Church, "'Tis So Sweet to Trust in Jesus," *The Continuing Witness*, http://www.thecontinuingwitness.com/uploads/9/8/2/3/98238342/tis_so_sweet_to_trust_in_jesus.pdf.

Chapter 8—Unattached and Unaffiliated: Uncompromised by Power

1. Shana Lynch, "The Dangers of Power," *Stanford Business*, July 27, 2016, https://www.gsb.stanford.edu/insights/dangers-power.

2. Arthur P. Boers, *Servants and Fools: A Biblical Theology of Leadership* (Nashville, TN: Abington Press, 2021), 143.

3. Brian Klaas, *Corruptible: Who Gets Power and How It Changes Us* (New York, NY: Scribner, 2021), 162.

4. Boers, *Servants and Fools*, 149.

Chapter 9—Discomfort: Freedom from Comfort

1. Peter Scazzero, *Emotionally Healthy Discipleship: Moving from Shallow Christianity to Deep Transformation* (Grand Rapids, MI: Zondervan, 2021), 90.

2. Dan B. Allender and Tremper Longman III, *Bold Love* (Colorado Springs, CO: NavPress, 1992), 205.

3. Amanda Lang, *The Beauty of Discomfort: How What We Avoid Is What We Need* (Toronto, ON: HarperCollins Canada, 2017), 49.

4. Shari Gootter and Tejpal, "What discomfort can teach you," *Counseling Today*, American Counseling Association, June 16, 2021, https://ct.counseling.org/2021/06/what-discomfort-can-teach-you.

5. Nathan Chandler, "How Geodesic Domes Work," How Stuff Works, September 13, 2011, https://science.howstuffworks.com/engineering/structural/geodesic-dome2.htm.

Chapter 10—Openhandedness: Generosity and Hospitality

1. John M. G. Barclay, *Paul and the Gift* (Grand Rapids, MI: Eerdmans Publishing Company, 2015), 41.

2. Timothy Keller, *Ministries of Mercy: The Call of the Jericho Road* (Phillipsburg, NJ: P & R Publishing, 1989), 66.

3. Craig L. Blomberg, *Christians in an Age of Wealth: A Biblical Theology of Stewardship* (Grand Rapids, MI: Zondervan Academic, 2013), 75.

4. Jessica Gross, "6 studies on how money affects the mind," *TED* (blog), December 20, 2013, https://blog.ted.com/6-studies-of-money-and-the-mind.

5. Gross, "6 studies on how money affects the mind."

6. Uma Shashikant, "Why poor people tend to be more gnerous than the rich," *Economic Times*, July 23, 2018, https://economictimes.indiatimes.com/wealth/save/why-poor-people-tend-to-be-more-generous-than-the-rich/articleshow/65078320.cms.

7. Herbert Scholssberg, *Idols for Destruction* (Nashville, TN: Nelson, 1983), 88-89.

8. Gerald H. Wilson, *Psalms Volume 1* (Grand Rapids, MI: Zondervan, 2002), 630.

9. Christine D. Pohl, *Making Room: Recovering Hospitality as a Christian Tradition* (Grand Rapids, MI: Eerdmans Publishing Company, 1999), 16.

Chapter 11—Endurance: The Persecuted Church

1. Alistair Begg, "Alistair Begg: 'Welcome to exile. It's going to be OK,'" *Gospel Coalition*, April 29, 2021, https://www.thegospelcoalition.org/article/exile-ok/.

2. Johnnie Moore, *The Martyr's Oath: Living for the Jesus They're Willing to Die For* (Carol Streams, IL: Tyndale House, 2001), 19.

3. Karen Ellis, "Who's Who: Three Groups of Thought on Persecution in America" (presentation, Liftin Symposium at Wheaton College, Wheaton, IL, November 7, 2022).

4. https://www.opendoors.org/en-US/persecution/methodology/.

5. Moore, *The Martyr's Oath*, 19.

6. SCI China correspondent, "439 Chinese Christian Leaders—and Counting—Sign Joint Statement Affirming Religious Freedom," *St. Charles Institute,*

September 5, 2018, https://www.stcharlesinstitute.org/voices/2018/9/4/198
-chinese-christian-leadersand-countingsign-public-joint-statement.

7. Alexander MacLaren, *MacLaren's Commentary: Expositions of Holy Scripture* (Fort Collins, CO: Delmarva Publications, Inc., 2013), n.p.

8. Stanley Hauerwas, *Matthew (Brazos Theological Commentary on the Bible)* (Ada, MI: Baker Publishing Group, 2007), 130.

Chapter 12—Suffering and Lament

1. Allie Jaynes, "Taiwan's most famous professional mourner," *BBC*, February 26, 2013, https://www.bbc.com/news/magazine-21479399.

2. Mark Vroegop, *Dark Clouds, Deep Mercy: Discovering the Grace of Lament* (Wheaton, IL: Crossway, 2019), 21.

3. Matthew Henry, *Short Comments on Every Chapter of the Holy Bible* (London: Religious Tract Society, 1839), 919.

4. Timothy Keller, *Walking with God through Pain and Suffering* (Westminster, London: Penguin Publishing Group, 2015), 175.

5. Esther Fleece, *No More Faking Fine: Ending the Pretending* (Grand Rapids, MI: Zondervan, 2017), 37.

6. Vroegop, *Dark Clouds, Deep Mercy*, 75.

7. Lionel Spencer Thornton, *The Common Life in the Body of Christ* (Westminster, United Kingdom: Dacrae Press, 1950), 36.

8. Glenn Packiam, "Five Things to Know About Lament," *N.T. Wright Online*, https://www.ntwrightonline.org/five-things-to-know-about-lament.

Chapter 13—Grief over Injustice

1. M. Daniel Carroll R., *Christians at the Border: Immigration, the Church, and the Bible* (Ada, MI: Baker Publishing, 2008), 102.

2. Ken Wytsma, *Pursuing Justice: The Call to Live and Die for Bigger Things* (Nashville, TN: Thomas Nelson, 2013), 6-8.

3. Claus Westermann, *Isaiah 40-66: A Commentary* (United Kingdom: Westminster Press, 1969), 356.

4. Scot McKnight, *The Letter of James* (Grand Rapids, MI: Eerdmans, 2011), 239.

Chapter 14—Becoming the Church of the Outsider

1. Brett McCracken, *Uncomfortable: The Awkward and Essential Challenge of Christian Community* (Wheaton, IL: Crossway , 2017), 214.

ACKNOWLEDGMENTS

I would not have imagined that a trip out to California for my former Indian American roommate's wedding would have landed me in a hotel lobby in a neighboring city sitting across from Karen Swallow Prior chatting casually about book ideas over breakfast, but sometimes life works out that way. Thank you, Karen, for nudging me to consider this topic a worthy and timely pursuit.

After completing a second book, I am even more convinced they are magic now than after finishing the first one. And that having really thoughtful community around to cheer you on, listen to half-formed ideas, ask if they can send you dinner when things get intense, or encourage you to step away from the keyboard when things get ugly is critical to staying sane. I am indebted to Courtney Ellis, Will Stockdale, and Juliet Vedral for the various ways they have gone above and beyond my expectations in encouraging me in this pursuit. I am grateful for your intervention, creativity, and affirmation of my gifts.

To those who helped me get my thoughts organized along the way—from outline to final edits—Beca Bruder, Chrissy Weeks, Christina Ko, Jessica Elliott, Traci Spackey, Letitia Harmon, Kara, and Mom, thank you for your input and patient listening ear. Many of you helped both emotionally and creatively throughout the process and I do not take your support for granted. You have cared for me well.

When I sent out the call for prayer, Kathy Kuhl, Alyssa Kroboth, Christina Eickenroht, Sarah Sawyer, Nana Dolce, Neann Mathai, Mazaré, Rebekah Schmerber, Jay Bethard, Anna Woofenden, and Katie Yoon answered. Knowing friends were praying for me was a boon.

Ruth Buchanan, having you in my circle was truly a lifeline. Thank you for your texts, understanding, wisdom, friendship, and for knowing how it all feels. I am also grateful for your early guidance as we brainstormed potential topics together.

Thank you, Professor Keene, for helping me find helpful resources for research, and to my other RTS professors who have encouraged me along the way, Professor Redd and Professor Lee. Your recognition of my gifts means more than you know.

Finally, thanks are due to my Harvest House team. There would be no words on the page had it not been for Kathleen Kerr. Thank you for believing in my voice and for greenlighting this project because it lit me up. I am grateful for the opportunity to put to the page ideas that have been brewing for a while. Last but definitely not least, Emma Saisslin, your expert editorial touch has made this work so much better, and I'm appreciative of your flexibility and patience throughout the process.

AUTHOR BIO

ALICIA J. AKINS is a writer who finds herself at home both nowhere and anywhere. Her interest in how differences can be our strengths has taken her across the globe, and after living and working in Asia for five years, she considers it a second home. She is a masters student at Reformed Theological Seminary, Washington, DC. You can find more of her writing at FeetCryMercy.com and follow her on Twitter @FeetCryMercy.

INVITATIONS
TO ABUNDANCE

How the Feasts of the Bible
Nourish Us Today

From Genesis through Revelation, redemptive history is captured through feasts. *Invitations to Abundance* brings alive the feasts of scripture—from the well known to the less familiar—and reveals how relevant they are in our modern world.